Introduction

Gardening is a hobby that offers fantastic rewards. But if you lack those vital green fingers, and suffer sleepless nights worrying that you've missed that crucial date for pruning roses or sowing carrots, fear not. Here's where the *Amateur Gardening Yearbook 2015* comes in.

With clear pictures and simple instructions, you have a comprehensive array of techniques, practical information and advice to give you better results. And we've included a bit of fun and trivia as well.

Each month there are checklists of jobs to do, along with a featured garden to visit, details of five plants in season, practical articles – and a Masterclass to show you special techniques for achieving spectacular results in a given area of the garden, from planning a veg patch and creating an alpine planter, to sowing hardy annuals and planting tropical containers.

Whether your horticultural preference is for the fruit, vegetable or ornamental garden, or you have specialist interests such as the greenhouse, rockery or pond, or maybe you are fanatical about your lawn... this book is for you. With the *Amateur Gardening Yearbook 2015*, we guarantee your fingers will turn a healthy shade of green!

Have a great gardening year!

Graham

GRAHAM CLARKE
EDITOR

Amateur Gardening is the UK's best-known weekly gardening magazine, and it is also the oldest, having been launched in 1884 and published continuously every week since. It leads on practical gardening information and its award-winning gardening news pages regularly break major stories. Expert columnists include Bob Flowerdew and Anne Swithinbank from radio's *Gardeners' Question Time*, and Peter Seabrook and Toby Buckland, both former presenters of TV's *Gardeners' World*. *Amateur Gardening* is on sale every Tuesday. For more details visit:

www.amateurgardening.com

Contents

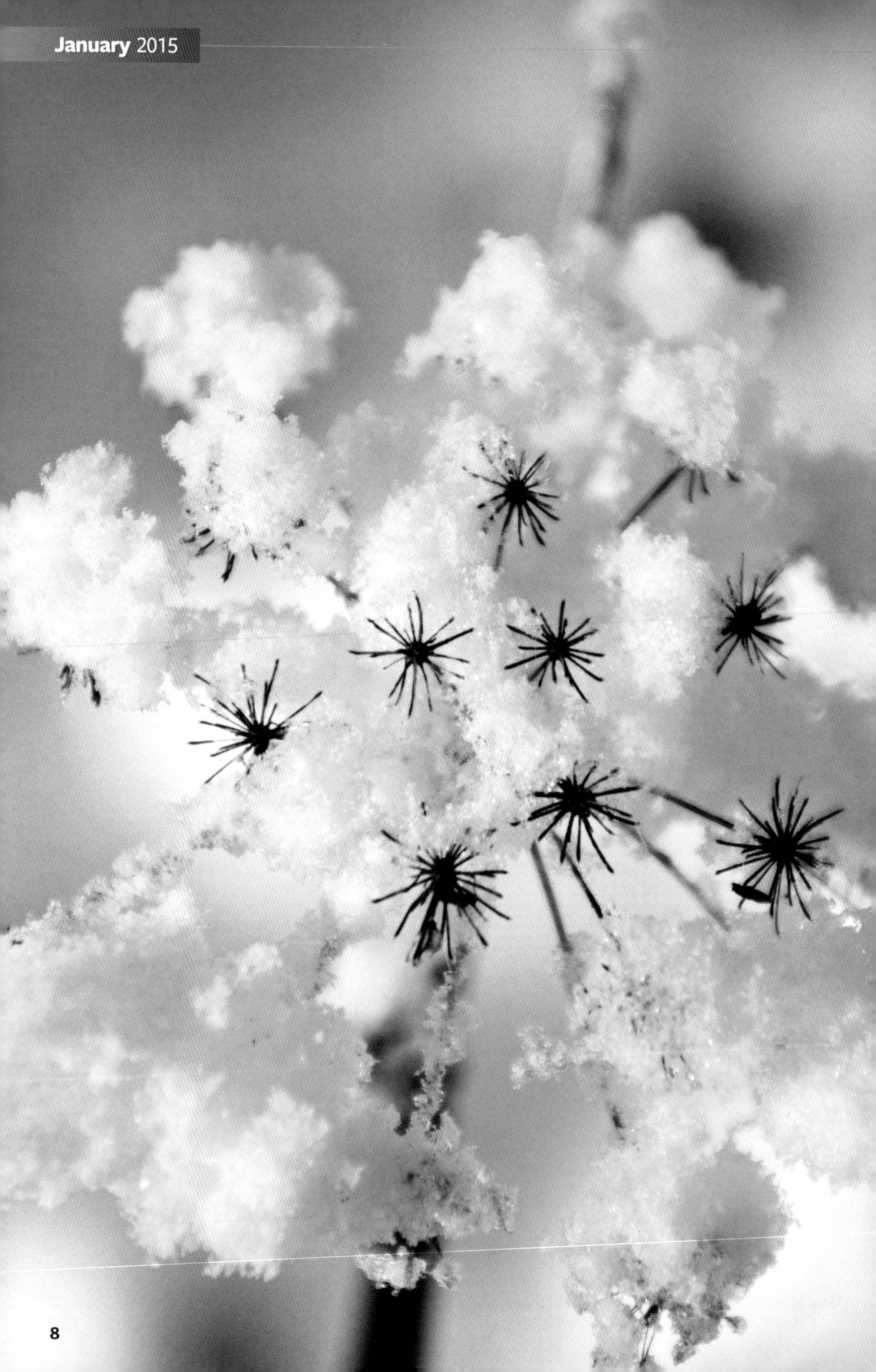

JANUARY

January marks a new year, and perhaps a new, fresh and vibrant start to the gardening year. Unfortunately the weather is not always conducive to this! Daytime temperatures during the month depend greatly on the direction of the wind; the warmth from the limited sunshine is too weak to make much difference.

But there is colour to be had in the garden in January: think of the bright reds of winter dogwood stems, the pinks and whites of winter heathers, and the yellows of winter jasmine. Enjoy, too, the silver foliage of stachys, the golden leaves of elaeagnus, and the wonderful shapes of all of the overwintering seedheads covered in a layer of frost.

January can be dark and gloomy, but in the garden our plants are doing all they can to make up for it.

◁ *A seedhead of geum (commonly known as avens), covered in January frost*

The garden in

January

GARDEN
TO
VISIT

Voted Britain's Favourite Garden in the BBC Countryfile Magazine Awards in 2013, this 240-acre (91ha) garden is the flagship garden of the Royal Horticultural Society. Famous for its richly planted borders, luscious rose gardens and the state-of-the-art glasshouse, in winter its woodland and heather gardens are a real feature.

HOW TO GET THERE: The garden is near Ripley in Surrey, off the main London to Portsmouth road (A3) south of Junction 10 of the M25. Follow the brown tourist flower signs on the A3 and M25. Car parking is free. For details of public transport, visit www.rhs.org.uk/Gardens and follow the links.

OPENING TIMES: Open every day except Christmas Day. Mon to Fri 10am – 4.30pm; Sat, Sun & Bank Holidays 9am – 4.30pm. Last admission one hour before closing.

RHS Garden
Wisley, Surrey
GU23 6QB

5 top plants for January

1 *Elaeagnus pungens* 'Gold Rim' provides a colourful splash of sunshine to the winter border.
2 *Lonicera fragrantissima* carries highly scented blooms in deep winter.
3 You can't beat the witch hazels for winter colour scent – this is *Hamamelis mollis* 'Imperialis'.
4 Another scented beauty is *Mahonia* 'Charity' with its bright yellow flower spikes and prickly leaves.
5 *Erica carnea* 'King George' is a low-grower with pink winter blooms that last for many weeks

This month in
Gardening
history

■ *1 JAN, 1946*
Britain's first-ever TV gardener, **Percy Thrower,** spent his first day as park's superintendent at Shrewsbury, Shropshire. He first appeared on TV in the 1950s and presented Gardeners' World from its beginning in 1969.

■ *10 JAN, 1778*
Carolus Linnaeus (*above*), Swedish botanist, died. He had developed the system for naming plants and animals in Latin.

■ *19 JAN, 1970*
The first **Gro-Bag** was launched by Fisons for the professional grower, and was followed by the launch of the consumer Gro-Bag four years later. Incredibly, some 12.5m are manufactured every year – the Levington Original remaining the best-selling branded bag.

JANUARY 2015

THURSDAY

1

FRIDAY

2

SATURDAY

3

SUNDAY

4

MONDAY

5

TUESDAY

6

WEDNESDAY

7

THURSDAY

8

AT A GLANCE
JOBS TO DO THIS MONTH

GENERAL TASKS

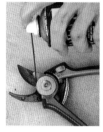

- [ ] Clean, sharpen and oil hand tools.
- [ ] Put the lawn mower in for a service.
- [ ] Spread organic matter over the borders and veg plot on dry days when the soil isn't frozen.
- [ ] Reflect on last year's successes and failures: decide whether there are any parts of the garden you want to change.
- [ ] On dry days, smarten up fences and with paint or preserver (*below*).

- [ ] Shred the Christmas tree and add to it to the compost heap.
- [ ] If fish ponds have frozen over; melt a small area of ice by sitting a hot pan on the surface for a few minutes.
- [ ] Provide birds with fresh water and food.
- [ ] Consider buying a water butt.

FLOWERS

- [ ] Order seed from mail order catalogues.
- [ ] Cut old leaves off hellebores.
- [ ] Order summer-flowering bulbs and perennials for planting in the spring.

JANUARY 2015

FRIDAY

9

SATURDAY

10

SUNDAY

11

MONDAY

12

TUESDAY

13

WEDNESDAY

14

THURSDAY

15

FRIDAY

16

Shred the Christmas tree and use the chippings in the garden – or take it to the green waste tip

Your notes

WEATHER:

PLANTS IN BLOOM:

TO DO:

JANUARY 2015

SATURDAY

17

SUNDAY

18

MONDAY

19

TUESDAY

20

WEDNESDAY

21

THURSDAY

22

FRIDAY

23

SATURDAY

24

AT A GLANCE
JOBS TO DO THIS MONTH

TREES, SHRUBS AND CLIMBERS

- Knock any snow off conifers, evergreens and hedges to avoid branches breaking.
- Order bare-root roses and plant out when soil conditions allow.

CONTAINERS AND PATIOS

- Deadhead pansies.
- Water any pots that may have dried out.
- Scrub slimy patches on the patio with a broom and detergent or pressure washer, if needed.

GREENHOUSE

- Wash down surfaces, pots and seed trays with hot water and mild detergent, rinse thoroughly.
- Install a water butt to catch roof run-off.
- Sow pelargonium, begonia and lobelia.
- Check stored dahlias and cannas; remove rotting ones.

WHAT TO PRUNE

✓ **Wisteria** – shorten summer-grown side shoots to two or three buds

✓ **Tidy ivies, Virginia creeper and climbing hydrangea** to prevent them from working their way into window frames and doors

JANUARY 2015

SUNDAY

25

MONDAY

26

TUESDAY

27

WEDNESDAY

28

THURSDAY

29

FRIDAY

30

SATURDAY

31

Your notes

WEATHER:

PLANTS IN BLOOM:

TO DO:

true or false?

Before turning to gardening, *Amateur Gardening's* organic guru, and regular panellist on radio's *Gardeners' Question Time*, Bob Flowerdew (*above*) once worked as a chicken giblet washer and frozen chicken packer.

(Answer at the bottom of page 23)

PLANT IT

Pot plant persistence

What should you do with all those Christmas plants that are starting to fade?

WITH THE heady scent of paperwhite narcissi, and the brilliant colours of poinsettias, gardeners certainly had a plant-packed few months. But now, many of these favourite and familiar Christmas pot plants are fading.

Some are going into a resting period, which is quite normal. The bulbs – paperwhites, hyacinths and amaryllis – all need to convert energy from their leaves, into stored nutrients within the bulb so they can flower again next year.

Winter cherry, cyclamen and poinsettias take a rest during the spring and summer and put energy into forming new buds or stems.

It seems a shame to even contemplate throwing away any of these plants – as garden centres would prefer us to do. With some care, it is quite possible to keep them going, and allow them to give another burst of colour.

If you can't look after them all, which should you choose to save? It's down to personal choice really, but some are rather more conducive to repeat flowering than others.

It seems a shame to throw all these away when they stop being colourful. You should be able to get them to put on a fresh display of flowers. But first you just have to decide which ones you want to keep!

Azalea

Remove the dead flowers and move plants to a cool room over January and February to encourage new buds to form. Feed weekly with a liquid fertiliser, high in potassium (such as tomato feed). Place outside in a shady spot for summer. Sink the pot into the ground to stop them drying out, and bring back indoors before the first frosts.

FYI
Pot azaleas are not hardy to start with! After Christmas indoors, harden them off before planting outside.

Cyclamen

With indoor cyclamen, wait until they stop flowering then reduce watering and stop feeding. Place in a cool, well-lit room until the spring, when they can be placed outside or in a greenhouse. Re-pot in July with fresh compost, keeping them moist throughout summer. Bring back indoors before the temperature drops in autumn.

Hyacinths

Once your hyacinth bulbs have finished flowering, and the flower stems have withered, cut them off at the base. Leave the foliage to replenish the bulb with energy. Feed fortnightly with a liquid, all-purpose fertiliser until the leaves die down. At this time remove the foliage, and plant the bulbs outside in the soil to grow naturally for next year.

Poinsettias

These are difficult: they'll lose their red bracts, leaving just the green foliage. After leaf fall, cut stems back to a healthy bud and let the plants rest, keeping them almost dry. Place on a tray with wet pebbles to maintain humidity, spray new foliage daily with clean water. Repot the plants in May, and feed with a general liquid houseplant fertiliser.

Amaryllis

Remove the faded flowers then allow the stem to die back before removing it at the base (leave an inch or so of stalk – be careful not to damage the growing point at the top of the bulb). Until September, water and feed weekly, using a balanced liquid feed. Place the bulbs, in their pots, outside in a shady position after the last frost of late spring.

Paperwhite narcissi

These bulbs are not hardy, and won't grow well if planted outdoors. When they stop flowering remove the faded blooms, and let the stem and leaves turn yellow. To flower again the leaves need to wither for six weeks or so (to feed nutrients back to the bulb). Keep outside in the shade over summer and bring back indoors before the first frosts.

SOW IT

Propagating pelargoniums

IF YOU are a bedding plant fanatic you'll be familiar with the ever popular pelargonium, often referred to as 'geranium' (but not to be confused with the hardy border types).

Well established plants for summer can be had by sowing pelargonium seeds as early in the season as possible. Sowing in warmth in January means the plants will be ready to put on a strong display soon after planting out in late May/ early June. If you sow much later you may not get flowers until August.

Fibrex Nurseries was of the UK's leading growers of pelargoniums, and they always put up a fantastic display at RHS Chelsea and/or Hampton Court Shows (main picture). These displays make a perfect showcase for the different types of flower.

To make sure pelargonium seeds germinate, they need to be in a propagator. If you don't have one you can still sow now, placing the seed trays/pots in clear plastic bags on a warm windowsill. Once sown keep them warm until planting out time in late May.

With a little heat, bedding geraniums can be sown in the depths of winter

FYI
Pelargonium seed is costly so chat with friends to see what they are growing, and swap seedlings in spring.

Pom-pom headed bedding pelargoniums are hugely popular; seek out a specialist nursery to discover the range available.

Notes and tips

Pelargonium 'Irene' is a bright zonal-leaved variety, perfect for bedding out.

Step *by* step ➤ Sowing pelargoniums in trays

1 Overfill pots or trays with a seed sowing compost. Gently tap the tray and level off the compost.

2 Before sowing the seeds, water the tray and allow the compost to drain and settle down.

3 Sow one seed into each cell, or scatter keeping the seeds 1in (2.5cm) apart. Press them in gently.

4 Cover with a fine layer of vermiculite, label and place into a propagator at 21-24°C (70-75°F).

On-going care

- **Remove lid/bag once the majority of seedlings have sprouted**

- Maintain a temperature of 18°C (64°F). Position in good light

- **Maintain good air circulation around the plants as pelargoniums are prone to greymould (botrytis) disease**

- Once large enough to handle by their first true leaves, pot on the seedlings individually into 3in (7.5cm) pots, or large cell trays

- **Give a fortnightly feed with a balanced fertiliser in spring**

- When flowers start to form, switch to a feed high in potash

'Ansbrook Venus', a 'Stellar' pelargonium

PRUNE IT

Winter fruit pruning

Prune your apple and pear trees now to boost fruit setting later in the season.

IT'S EASY to blame the weather, or pests or diseases, for your apple and pear trees failing to produce a good crop. However, the real reason may be due to something completely under your control – pruning (or lack of).

Good pruning creates an open framework, allowing air to circulate around the branches, which can reduce the risk of fungal infections. Correctly pruned trees will put on new, healthy growth, which in turn will produce new fruiting buds.

Winter pruning should be carried out between November and March, before 'bud burst', while the tree is still dormant. The best time is Jan-early Feb, when swollen buds are easy to spot, enabling you to position the cuts correctly.

Before starting, assess the tree to determine if it produces fruit on tips or spurs. Apple trees can be tip-bearing, spur-bearing, or both. Pears are mostly spur-bearing, but there are a few tip-bearers.

How much you cut out will depend on the age of the tree. Follow the tips on these pages to help you identify how your tree grows its fruit, and how to prune branches correctly.

FYI
For large jobs, and trees needing major work, it's best to call in a tree surgeon. Check their qualifications first though.

Pruning apple trees (along with pear and crab apple trees) will improve fruit production, the health of the trees, and their shape

Pruning spur-bearers

- Fruit is formed on 'spurs' of wood, created over two years or more. The main objective when pruning these types of trees is to encourage the growth of more fruiting spurs.
- On older apple and pear trees, prune out congested spurs and any badly placed ones (*left*).
- Shorten last year's growth by about two-thirds. Always cut to a bud facing in the direction you want the new growth to grow.
- Cut back young, vigorous sideshoots from the main framework to five or six buds. This is where fruit will form.

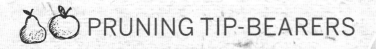 PRUNING TIP-BEARERS

- With these trees, the fruit is formed at or near the tip of the previous year's growth. Therefore it is important to leave some branches un-pruned (so they produce fruit). At the same time, new growth must be encouraged to produce fruiting buds for the year after.

- Prune new growth on branch leaders by one third, to an outward facing bud *(pic top right)*.

- Do not prune lateral branches which have fruit buds on, as these will produce the fruit for the coming season. Fruit buds are much fatter than forming shoot buds, *(pic bottom right)*.

- Prune any laterals with shoot buds (not fruit buds), back to three or four buds. This will encourage the growth of fruiting buds for the next year.

Basic pruning rules (for all trees)

1. Step back and look at the tree shape before deciding which branches to prune and which ones to leave alone.

2. Prune out damaged and diseased branches first.

3. Cut out crossing *(see pic)* and congested stems to create an open framework in the shape of a goblet.

4. Take your time: keep stepping back to note the shape of the tree whilst pruning.

5. Don't over-reach and risk a fall. Use a sturdy stepladder when necessary, and ideally have someone on hand to steady it.

6. Use clean, sharp tools that are fit for purpose, and clean them between jobs.

Which tools to use?

Pruning effectively 'wounds' the tree so it is vital the correct tools are used to keep damage to a minimum, and to ensure the tree heals quickly. Clean tools between major cuts, and between different trees, and ensure that the blades are sharp (to achieve clear, clean cuts).

- Secateurs: These are the best to use on young trees, on branches that are easily reached, and those of ¾ in (2cm) or less in diameter. Bypass blades are best, *(right)*. They perform a slicing motion, like scissors.

- Lopping shears are great to cut through branches less than 1½in (4cm). They have long handles giving you extra reach when pruning more mature trees. Use loppers with shock absorbing bumpers in between handles to lessen arm fatigue.

- Pruning saws remove stems that are too thick to be cut with loppers or secateurs. They can come in many sizes with straight or curved blades. Choose a fine-toothed saw for branches less than 2.5in (6cm). A coarse toothed saw is quicker when pruning branches 3in (7.5cm) or more in diameter.

Masterclass

January

Plan your veg patch

Plan now to make sure you get what you want from your plot

KEEPING A veg plot productive and looking good all year round requires planning. And because now is a quiet time (digging is done, not much to sow, and weed growth is slow), it's a great time to plan ahead. Best of all, it can be done indoors!

But to achieve a year-round productive and aesthetically pleasing plot, there are many things to consider. Where do you start? Hopefully the sequence of events below will set you on the right path.

Winter is a good time to plan where your beds will be sited – and what you will grow in them

Choose varieties and order seeds

You should not delay in selecting and ordering your varieties of choice. There may be new strains just introduced, or tried and trusted ones that you simply don't want to miss. The sooner you make your selection, and place your order, the better the chance that you will get what you want, and stock will not have run out.

JANUARY

S	M	T	W	T	F	S
				1	2	3
4	5	6	7	8	9	10
11	12	13	14	15	16	17
18	19	20	21	22	23	24
25	26	27	28	29	30	31

Burn's Night

Order seeds

Do you currently have a veg plot?

 YES You have a plot where you've grown veg for one or more years. To avoid a disease build-up, don't to grow the same crops on the same part of the plot over succeeding years.

Do you follow a crop rotation plan?

If not, start now. Group separately potatoes, peas and beans, brassicas and root crops, and divide the plot into four distinct growing areas. Each veg group is moved one area forward each year: brassicas (cabbages, caulis, broccoli, sprouts and swedes) follow peas and beans; peas and beans follow root crops; root crops follow potatoes; potatoes follow brassicas – and the cycle repeats.

What were the successes in your veg plot in 2014?

You may want to revise the types of crop you grow, or the way you grow them. The kind of questions to ask yourself, and points to consider, include:

- **Tomatoes** – do you want to grow them in pots or bags on hard ground or in the greenhouse, or try them in the soil?

- **Carrots** – were yours 'forked'? If so, it could be because of stony soil, or there was too much rich manure in the soil.

 NO You have a garden, but have never grown vegetables before; or you may just have taken over an allotment for the first time.

Have you marked out the ground?

If not already done, you'll need to measure off and mark out the area, and then dig it over. Don't delay in doing this, particularly if your soil is clay (the winter frosts break up the clods making the soil much easier to work). Choose a day when the ground is neither waterlogged nor frosted. Dig the plot, two spade blades deep if possible, working in rows. Add well-rotted manure or compost at all levels. If converting lawn, remove the top couple of inches and stack the turf in a pile to rot down.

Have you considered raised beds?

These can be made yourself (*see main picture opposite*), or are available by mail order and from some garden centres. They have rigid sides so that you can build up a depth of soil within them. This makes the bed easier to maintain if you find it difficult to stoop, or want to grow the deeper root crops.

TRUE OR FALSE FROM p15: **TRUE.** Bob started off as the former, and was promoted to the latter!

FEBRUARY

One feature of the climate that is important in February is the soil temperature. It is often the ultimate decider as to whether the spring is early or late. Soil temperatures are always at their lowest in early February, and will likely be below average if there has been a succession of nights with hard frosts and no snow cover.

If the winter has been wet so far, and especially if the previous summer has also been rainy, and lacking in sunshine, then it is wise at the end of February to check the pH and nitrogen levels of the soil to see if extra feeding in spring is necessary.

Plants of note in February include the early magnolias, witch hazels, mahonias, shrubby honeysuckles and the highly fragrant daphnes.

◁ *In the depths of winter, a hanging basket or patio container can be filled with cheerful plants.*

The garden in
February

GARDEN TO VISIT

An oasis of peace and tranquillity at any time of year, in February pure white snowdrops are usually a major feature. Discover the Secret Garden, a plantsman's paradise hidden within ancient walls. Naturalistic plantings give a modern flavour to a traditional Victorian garden complete with box hedges. In spring and summer, lilacs and roses abound. In autumn, grasses sway in the breeze, catching the low sun. A burn runs gently towards the sea. The garden offers respite from a busy world.

HOW TO GET THERE: The garden is on the A917 just South of St Andrews in the East of Fife, Scotland. Edinburgh is approximately a 1 hour drive. For details of public transport, visit www.camboestate.com and follow the links.

OPENING TIMES: Open daily. 10am – 5pm. Weekly tours every Tuesday at 1pm.

Cambo Gardens, St. Andrews, Fife KY16 8QD

5 top plants for February

1 *Helleborus niger* (the Christmas rose) is not a rose, and it doesn't bloom at Christmas – but it is a beauty.
2 *Cornus sericea* 'Flaviramea' produces wonderful acid yellow stems in winter.
3 The alpine *Primula allionii* 'Elizabeth Earle'.
4 A highly scented form of wintersweet – *Chimonanthus praecox* var. *luteus*.
5 *Crocus oliveri* subsp *balansai* 'Zwanenburg' is one of the brightest and most reliable of the winter-blooming crocus.

This month in
Gardening
history

■ *6 FEB 1783*
Sir Lancelot 'Capability' Brown, landscaper, died. Famously he designed and was instrumental in creating more than 170 parks, many of which still exist. He is remembered by many as "England's greatest gardener".

■ *25 FEB, 1966*
Levington Compost, for both professional grower and amateur gardener, was launched. An all-round growing medium, it is a unique combination of peat, sterilised loam and horticultural sand.

■ *16 FEB, 1926*
David Charles Henshaw Austin (*above*), arguably the most famous rose breeder (and owner of the nursery named after him), was born. Every year his nursery launches a range of new varieties.

FEBRUARY 2015

SUNDAY

1

MONDAY

2

TUESDAY

3

WEDNESDAY

4

THURSDAY

5

FRIDAY

6

SATURDAY

7

SUNDAY

8

AT A GLANCE
JOBS TO DO THIS MONTH

GENERAL TASKS

- Buy or order plug plants (*below*).
- Finish off winter digging/manuring.
- Create new beds and borders to make way for any new design plans.
- Provide food for birds – it's a very hungry month for wildlife.

LAWNS

- Mow lawns if mild and dry, keeping blades high, and prepare ground for a new lawn if required.

TREES, SHRUBS AND CLIMBERS

- Plant bare-root trees and shrubs and move deciduous woody plants.
- Take hardwood cuttings (these can actually be taken anytime between mid-autumn and late winter).
- Cut back dogwood hard, for colourful stems next winter (*below*).

FEBRUARY 2015

MONDAY

9

TUESDAY

10

WEDNESDAY

11

THURSDAY

12

FRIDAY

13

SATURDAY

14

SUNDAY

15

MONDAY

16

February is the time to winter-prune wisteria

Your notes

WEATHER:

PLANTS IN BLOOM:

TO DO:

FEBRUARY 2015

TUESDAY

17

WEDNESDAY

18

THURSDAY

19

FRIDAY

20

SATURDAY

21

SUNDAY

22

MONDAY

23

TUESDAY

24

AT A GLANCE
JOBS TO DO THIS MONTH

 **FLOWERS**

- [ ] Plant out pot-grown spring bulbs and polyanthus for instant colour (harden off first).
- [ ] Tidy and deadhead winter pansies (*right*).
- [ ] Start off dahlia tubers in trays or pots.
- [ ] Add some winter colour to borders.
- [ ] Divide snowdrops after flowering.
- [ ] Order summer bulbs for spring planting.

IN THE GREENHOUSE

- [ ] Sow sweet peas, lobelia, begonias, impatiens and pelargonium.

 CONTAINERS AND PATIOS

- [ ] Water and top-dress plants in long-term permanent pots.
- [ ] Treat yourself to a winter-flowering scented shrub in a pot like *Sarcococca confusa* (plant out into the garden after a couple of years).

WHAT TO PRUNE

- ✓ Winter jasmine
- ✓ *Buddleja davidii*
- ✓ Deciduous ceanothus
- ✓ Hardy fuchsias
- ✓ Late-flowering clematis
- ✓ Ornamental grasses
- ✓ Leycesteria
- ✓ Trim winter heathers as flowers fade
- ✓ Last chance to prune wisteria

FEBRUARY 2015

WEDNESDAY

25

THURSDAY

26

FRIDAY

27

SATURDAY

28

Your notes

WEATHER:

PLANTS IN BLOOM:

TO DO:

true or false?

Many viewers of gardening on TV will be fans of celebrity gardeners Carol Klein and Christine Walkden. However, strangely, Christine (*right*) was born in a village called... Klein!

(Answer at the bottom of page 41)

PLANT IT

Baskets makeover

Refresh winter pots and baskets ready for spring

THE SEASONAL hanging baskets and containers created back in autumn may now have succumbed to winter wet. The constant damp atmosphere and large amounts of rainfall have caused saturated soil, resulting in plant losses and a few pest and disease problems. Pansies may be suffering from leaf spot. Slugs will have taken their toll, too.

New bedding plants and spring bulbs can be picked up cheaply, so there's little point in keeping plants that have been affected by pests and diseases, at the risk of spreading problems to other plants.

Some winter plants are better able to survive. *Carex* 'Frosted Curls', ivy and cineraria can all tough it out, looking good and healthy. These can remain – just replace those around them.

Late winter and early spring can still take their toll on young flowers; buy varieties that will tolerate late frosts, and have some fleece to hand to protect them if needed.

Winter rain will likely have flushed out the nutrients from container composts, so remove the top 2in (5cm) and replace with fresh compost, and start feeding fortnightly. Follow the tips on these pages and you could soon bring displays back to life.

Wet winter weather can cause container displays to lose their shine. Adding spring blooms will inject colour back into the scene

Step by step — Bringing colour to your winter displays

1 Decide which plants can stay in your displays and tie these back, using an old hair band or string, to give you better access to the plants around them.

2 Remove all old, diseased and dead plants that you want to replace, taking care not to damage or cut into the roots of the plants you want to keep.

3 Scrape away as much compost as possible, without disturbing or damaging the remaining plants. Use hands or a small trowel to do this. Replace with same compost.

Pansy leaf spot

Pansies and violas can be attacked by fungal pathogens, causing spots and marks on their leaves (*below*). Try the ideas here, to reduce the spread.

- **Remove promptly and destroy diseased plants**
- Do not plant new pansies or violas in the same site
- **Scrape away and dispose of the top layer of soil**
- Fungicides may work, but none are marketed for controlling leaf spot diseases. Try Fungus Clear Ultra or Plant Rescue Fungus Control
- **Check over new plants before buying; do not buy any with signs of fungal infections**

Replacement plants

Bedding

- **Primula**
- Pansy
- **Viola (*right*)**
- Cyclamen

Bulbs

- **Narcissus**
- Anemone
- **Snake's head fritillary**
- Iris reticulata (*left*)
- **Crocus**
- Snowdrops
- **Tulip**
- Hyacinth

Foliage

- **Ornamental cabbage (*right*)**
- Evergreen grasses
- **Ivy**
- Ferns

4 To save money and spread new colour across the display, separate plants and bulbs across the pots. Prise apart gently, making sure each plant has good roots.

5 Set the new plants in their places, adding multipurpose compost to fill spaces. Really pack the pot/basket full with plants for extra impact.

6 Untie the existing plants and tidy by removing dead leaves and flowers. Ornamental grasses can be trimmed or combed through to remove dead foliage.

Blueberries in containers

If you don't have the right soil for blueberries, don't worry!

A LOT of claims are made about the 'superfruit' on a blueberry bush: high nutrient and vitamin levels, high in antioxidants, anti-cancer properties... the list goes on. But for most of us, we just like the blueberry taste, and that's why we grow them.

Fruiting aside, blueberries make a decorative addition to the garden, particularly in autumn when the leaves turn from green through shades of red, purple and yellow. And the bell-like flowers make a strong statement in spring, too.

However if your soil is neutral to alkaline you won't have much success with these acid-loving plants. If you have heavy clay, or limey soil, adjusting its acidity can be difficult, and the prepared area can quickly lose the acidity you add to it as well. So your best chance of growing blueberries is to set them in pots filled with ericaceous compost. Late Feb/March is the best time to plant them, giving them a full season of growth before facing up to a cold winter outside.

FYI
Get the most from your ericaceous pots: underplant blueberries with acid-loving cranberries.

Pot on each spring in slightly larger pots

Give your berries a boost

Blueberries don't need a pollinating partner to fruit, so if you're short on space just plant one. However, grow two or more plants close to each other and both will crop heavier than if stood alone. All varieties flower around the same time, but fruits ripen at different times according to variety.

A top variety is 'Pink Lemonade' which produces unusual pink berries (*right*) in August and Sept.

Potting guide

- Blueberries prefer an annual repotting. They take around eight years to mature, and should go into slightly larger pots  each year until you reach an eventual pot diameter of 3ft (90cm).

- Each spring choose a weather-proof pot a few inches wider than the existing pot.

- **Line the base with an inch or so of grit/gravel for drainage.**

- Add a few inches of ericaceous compost to the bottom, so that when placed, the top of the root ball is just below the pot rim.

- **Pack around the rootball with more compost (*above*), firming down as you go.**

- Apply a topdressing of grit/gravel to help retain moisture and prevent weed growth.

- **Water to settle in, but only use rain water.**

Notes and tips

Pancakes are always a favourite with children. Add blueberries to them to give them one of their seven a day!

TIPS FOR SUCCESS

 Potting up is best done in early spring. If an existing plant has been sitting in its original pot, in the garden, since the previous autumn, pot it up now.

 Apply an ericaceous feed each April to help with fruit development.

3 Use rain water when possible (*below*). Tap water contains lime which will raise the pH level within the compost over time.

4 Blueberries fruit on last year's growth, and older. No pruning is needed in the first three years, although removing stem tips on plants with few side shoots should encourage bushier growth early on.

5 Place netting over plants as fruit ripens, to prevent losing it to hungry birds.

SOW IT

Leaf bedding to sow now

Colourful summer leaves are just as attractive as flowers!

FLORAL SUMMER bedding plants have many uses in the garden, but for a more dramatic effect they need planting partners that offer contrast or bring an extra element to the display. As I pick my summer bedding varieties to grow from seed, I always have an eye out for vibrant foliage plants that can be sown and grown alongside the summer bloomers to add strong colour or contrast.

Half hardy annual foliage plants can be used in the same way as traditional flowering bedding – in containers, baskets and as border fillers. Many perform well in shade, making them perfect plants for problem spots in the garden. Growing these foliage plants from seed will save you money, and sowing now, means that they will soon germinate to reach a good size in time for planting out after the last of the spring frosts.

Here are some top choices, and sowing tips to enhance your summer bedding displays.

FYI
Bring a few of these foliage bedding plants indoors in autumn to brighten up the home during the cooler months.

An early sowing of these great foliage plants means they will be ready to plant out in late spring

Leafy combinations

Silver-leaved plants go with almost anything, but particularly with dark red: so try silver cineraria with maroon coleus!

Bright yellow (as with some of the miniature bedding conifers) goes with dark green (say, with a sea of deep variegated ivy).

Grow multicoloured amaranthus with white-fowered petunias.

Foliage to grow from seed

■ *Dichondra argentea*
'Silver Falls'
(from T&M, *below*) With its trailing foliage, this plant looks stunning in pots and baskets.

■ **Coleus**
Available in many bright colours (*above*), great in borders to add colour

■ **Kale 'Ornamental Peacock'**
Vibrant purple stems and foliage (*below*), looks great in containers and borders (Available from Suttons)

■ *Cineraria* **'Silver Dust'**
A great filler plant that looks amazing in baskets, borders and pots (*above*).

■ *Colocasia fallax*
(silver leaf elephant ear) Leaves are green, with silver markings. Available from Chiltern Seeds
@ www.chilternseeds.co.uk
📞 01491 824675

■ *Amaranthus tricolor*
'Joseph's Coat'
Yellow and scarlet leaves win over its flowers. Looks fantastic in borders for a warm display

How to sow

- **Fill either pots or trays with sieved seed compost**
- Water the compost and allow to drain and settle
- **Sow the seeds evenly on the surface of the compost**
- Most foliage seeds need light to sprout, so only cover very lightly with compost
- **To maintain humidity, cover with a plastic bag (*right*) or place in a heated propagator**
- Place on or near a windowsill at a temperature of 20-25°C (70-75°F) for germination
- **Thin out seedlings when large enough to handle**
- Transplant young plants into 3in (7.5cm) pots or modules
- **Plant out when all risk of frost has passed**

PLANT IT

Planting roses in the garden

Bare-root, pre-packed and pot roses are all available in Feb, so get planting

ROSES ARE versatile plants: they're easy to look after and will grow pretty much anywhere (barring the sandiest of soils, and as long as they are placed in a sunny position, sheltered from strong winds, with plenty of room and food).

Choose the right site and you will be rewarded with healthy, strong growth, and years of garden colour.

Avoid planting new roses where roses have been grown in the past. Doing so may cause the new plants to suffer from 'rose-sickness'. Symptoms include sluggish growth, and increased susceptibility to diseases. You can use the same space for roses if you replace the soil to a depth of 18in (45cm) before planting.

It is best to plant roses before the end of March, to give them time to settle and establish before the summer flowering starts.

Roses love soils rich in organic matter. Mixing in well-rotted manure a few weeks prior to planting will give them everything they need for good, early growth.

There is no need to add extra fertiliser to the planting hole, providing plenty of organic matter has been added. But, to maintain vigour, feed through the year. So get to it, and plant a rose this spring.

FYI
When handling, planting or pruning traditional thorny-stemmed roses, always wear stout gloves!

This border already holds a few roses, but with careful planning and selection of varieties, even more can go in for a great summer display

Roses are versatile plants, use them in:

- **Formal bedding schemes**
- Mixed borders
- **Hedging**
- Containers
- **Up walls and fences**
- As a focal point in gardens

How to plant roses

1 **Prepare the site a few weeks prior to planting by** digging in well-rotted manure, at least a bucketful to every square yard (square metre)

2 Soak bare-root and wrapped roses in a bucket of water for a couple of hours before planting

3 **Container roses need to be watered at least an** hour before planting

4 With bare-rooted types, dig a hole wide enough for the roots to be spread out

5 **With container grown and pre-wrapped roses, tease** out roots before planting

6 Plant the rose in the centre of the hole, making sure the graft is at soil level. This is seen as a bulge at the base (*see picture below*)

7 **Backfill with soil and gently firm the rose in** with the heel of your foot

8 On poor soils apply a general fertiliser around the base of the plant at 3oz per sq yd (80g per sq m) and lightly fork in, avoiding roots

9 **If planting more than one rose, spacing will depend** on the variety – check labels

10 For standard roses, hammer in a tree stake at an angle of 45 degrees.

Know your roses

Standard roses
Many roses can be grown as a standard (with a long, clear stem). Good for using to add height to borders, and can be underplanted. However they do need some support – a tree post and tie is best.

Bush roses
These roses have upright growth with large flowers. They usually have one flower per stem. Many varieties produce a second flush later in the year. Ideal in borders.

Climber and rambler roses
Climbers and ramblers have strong upright growth, great for training on walls, fences and trellis. Rambling roses (not all) usually flower just once, while climbers tend to repeat flower.

Patio roses
These roses were bred to combat the problem of many older style roses failing in container displays due to restricted root growth. These smaller plants are ideal for patios or balconies.

Modern shrub roses
Also known as the English rose (made popular by breeder David Austin), they are a cross between modern and old varieties. They usually have strong scent, with the repeat flowering habit of 'old roses'.

February

Masterclass

Moving large shrubs

Hazel

Spindle

Amateur Gardening editor **Tim Rumball** transplants shrubs in his garden

This is the main border in my back garden. The contorted hazel is to go, and the spindle will move across into its place. The evergreen shrubs behind will be pruned back in spring

T HE SHRUBS in the main border of my back garden became too big, and started to crowd one another out. Some needed pruning, one needed moving, and one – the contorted hazel (which my wife Kath fell out-of-love with) had to be removed.

If you've got big deciduous shrubs to move it's OK to do it until the end of February – the plants should still be dormant. But be warned, it's heavy work.

The main picture above shows, to the right of me, the condemned contorted hazel. And far right is the winged spindle (*Euonymus alatus*), which needed moving into the space.

Digging out the hazel was heavy going. At about 10 years old, it had put down deep roots. I wasn't planning to keep the plant, but I needed the roots out to make room for the spindle. Removing the hazel was tough, but nothing compared to the blood (I cut my finger), sweat and tears (of frustration) I endured when shifting the spindle. The rootball took some heaving!

Once I'd freed it, I tore strips off an old sheet to make broad straps to tie around it to give me something to hold. Then brute force was needed to heave the plant out of the hole. You could lift it onto a tarpaulin, but I didn't have one.

The straps, and a couple of planks to skate it along, helped me to wrestle the spindle into its new home. Soil was carefully tucked around the roots then thumped down with gloved hands to firm it and remove air pockets. Watering was unnecessary as it was raining heavily by then, but I'll water it whenever there are dry spells. Tall shrubs would need staking, but my spindle is a low grower.

One branch broke in the move, and I've bandaged it up in the hope it will mend.

The worst job done, now I've just got the pruning of evergreens in spring – and a new space to plant up with perennials!

Removing the top growth of the hazel, I left one sturdy trunk to give me leverage. Digging and pulling soon broke the roots free.

Then over to the spindle. I dug a trench 18in (45cm) deep around the rootball, using the edge of the plant's canopy as a guide.

Next I undercut the rootball, as far as I could reach. I used a spade for this, to chop away and dig out the soil beneath.

Broad strips of sheet were used as slings around the rootball. These meant I had 'handles' to pull it out.

FEBRUARY

S	M	T	W	T	F	S
				1	2	3
4	5	6	7	8	9	10
11	12	13	14	15	16	17
18	19	20	21	22	23	24
25	26	27	28	29	30	31

Valentine's Day

Move shrub

I dug and prepared the new planting hole, then slid the plant up a pair of smooth planks. I settled it, then firmed it in place.

TRUE OR FALSE FROM p31: **FALSE**. Christine was *not* born in Klein, however in 1945 Carol *was* born in the Lancashire village of...Walkden!

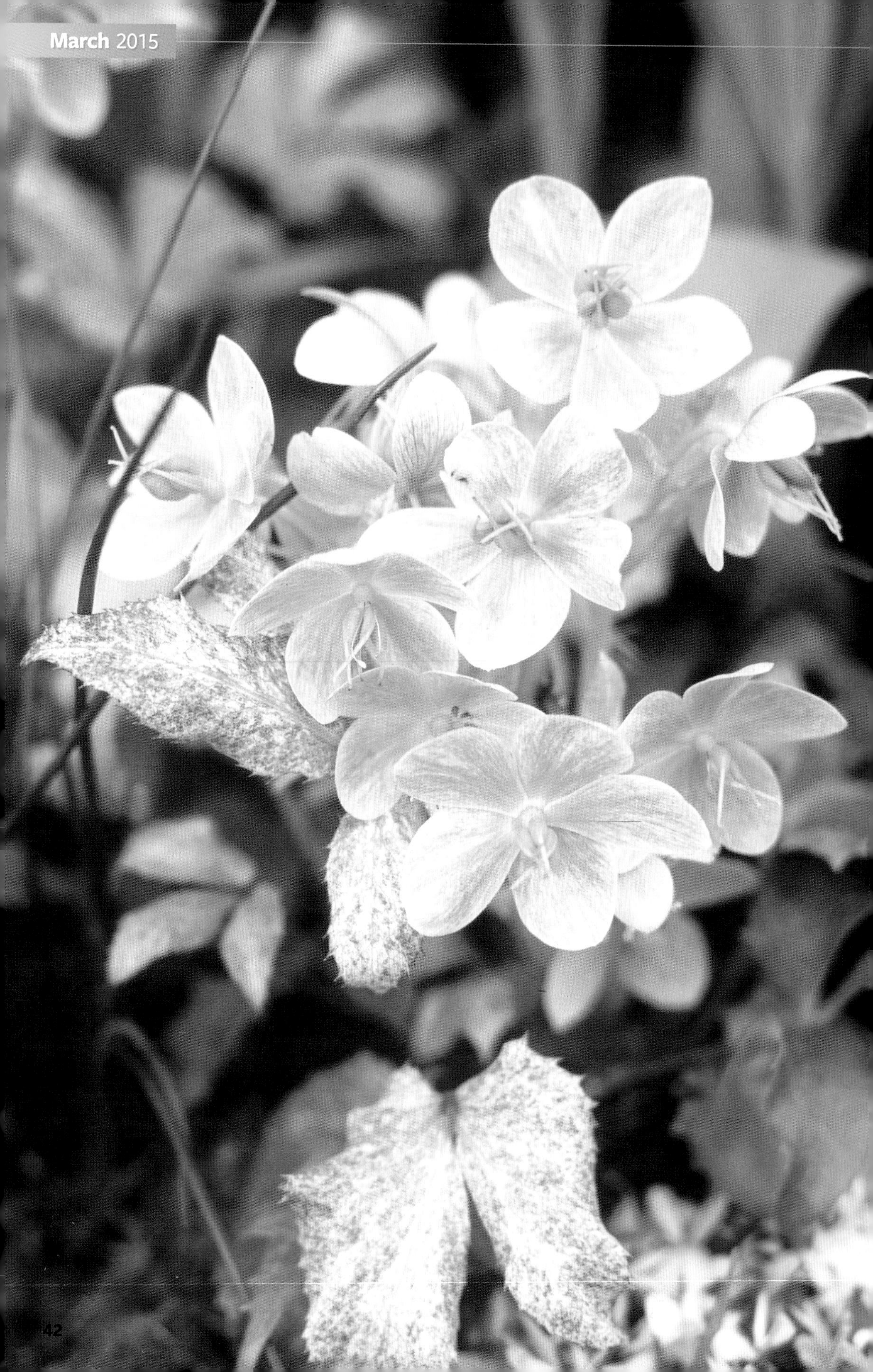

MARCH

March is traditionally supposed to come in like a lion and go out like a lamb, or vice versa. However, this is not always true as far as strong winds are concerned. It is better to consider the month as simply being, in most years, the first real signs of spring.

Spring in the garden comes earliest in the far south-west, and latest in the north-east, with the western coastal regions always being ahead of the east.

Remember that a successful garden also depends on "March winds and April showers": the purpose of the winds is to help dry out the top layers of the seedbed so that the gardener can create a good 'tilth' (a crumbly soil surface into which seeds can be sown and germinated).

Many spring bulbs (including daffodils, crocus, hyacinths and so on) are looking their best now. Camellias, Japanese quince, forsythia and *Viburnum tinus* are looking good in the shrub border.

◁ *Hellebores are a strong feature of woodland and flower borders between Christmas and spring. This is Helleborus argutifolius 'Pacific Frost'*

The garden in *March*

GARDEN TO VISIT

This 360-acre (145ha) garden is a Royal Horticultural Society property in an area of Essex that has very low rainfall. This factor, combined with the soil conditions and exposed nature of the site, makes it a challenging area for gardening. A favourite feature is the Dry Garden, which showcases a fantastic range of drought-tolerant plants; in recent years it has doubled in size.

HOW TO GET THERE: The garden is just 20 minutes from the centre of Chelmsford and is signposted from the A130 (southbound). Car parking is free. For details of public transport, visit www.rhs.org.uk/Gardens and follow the links.

OPENING TIMES: Open every day except Christmas Day. Nov-Feb: 10am – 4pm; Mar-Oct: 10am – 6pm. Last admission one hour before closing.

RHS Garden Hyde Hall, Essex CM3 8ET

5 top plants for March

1 *Primula* Gold Lace Black has a golden centre, black outer petals and gold picotee edge.
2 *Aubrieta deltoidea* 'Doctor Mules' is perfect for a sunny rockery or top of a wall.
3 *Iris reticulata* 'Harmony' is one of the prettiest, and most vibrant of the dwarf spring bulb irises.
4 The forsythia (or 'golden bells' is commonly seen in spring gardens; this is *F*. x *intermedia* 'Spectabilis'.
5 Hyacinth 'Midnight Mystique' is one of the darkest available.

This month in
Gardening
history

■ *2 MAR 1921*
Christopher Lloyd
(*below*) gardener and author, was born. He owned Great Dixter in Sussex, and was the 20th Century chronicler for the heavily planted, labour-intensive, country garden. He died in 2006.

■ *9 MAR, 1892*
Vita Mary Sackville-West
was born. A famous socialite and writer, she famously owned Sissinghurst in Kent, now a National Trust house and garden. She died in 1962.

■ *22 MAR, 1915*
Tomorite tomato fertiliser, used by millions of gardeners every year to promote flowers and fruit on a wide range of plants, was launched (originally in solid form – now in liquid).

45

MARCH 2015

SUNDAY

1

MONDAY

2

TUESDAY

3

WEDNESDAY

4

THURSDAY

5

FRIDAY

6

SATURDAY

7

SUNDAY

8

AT A GLANCE
JOBS TO DO THIS MONTH

 ### GENERAL TASKS

☐ Spruce up the garden – fork over borders, hoe weeds, and cut back dead perennial stems left over the winter.

☐ Mulch the bare earth around plants with well-rotted manure if you haven't already done this in Jan/Feb.

LAWNS

☐ Begin regular mowing and edging the lawn (*right*), on dry days.

☐ Lay turf as the soil begins to warm, if you didn't in autumn.

CONTAINERS AND PATIOS

☐ Plant/freshen up seasonal containers with spring bedding, small evergreens and compact perennials; use John Innes No3 compost in long-term containers, multipurpose in short-term ones.

☐ Spruce up the patio by giving it a good scrub and removing moss and weeds

 ### FLOWERS

☐ Support herbaceous perennials.

☐ Sow hardy annuals.

☐ Divide overcrowded perennials.

☐ Divide/plant snowdrops in the green (*pictured*).

☐ Plant summer-flowering bulbs.

MARCH 2015

MONDAY

9

TUESDAY

10

WEDNESDAY

11

THURSDAY

12

FRIDAY

13

SATURDAY

14

SUNDAY

15

MONDAY

16

Plant gladioli corms now

Your notes

WEATHER:

PLANTS IN BLOOM:

TO DO:

MARCH 2015

TUESDAY

17

WEDNESDAY

18

THURSDAY

19

FRIDAY

20

SATURDAY

21

SUNDAY

22

MONDAY

23

TUESDAY

24

AT A GLANCE
JOBS TO DO THIS MONTH

 ### IN THE GREENHOUSE

☐ Sow sweet peas if you didn't manage to do it in January or February.

☐ Pot up plug plants and young plants after delivery or purchase.

☐ Repot cacti and succulents.

☐ Start off dahlias if you didn't last month; take cuttings from sprouting tubers. On cold nights cover vulnerable plants with newspaper or fleece.

 ### TREES, SHRUBS AND CLIMBERS

☐ Last chance to get bare-root plants into the soil, and to move deciduous trees and shrubs.

☐ This is also a good month to transplant evergreen shrubs.

☐ Plant new climbers.

WHAT TO PRUNE

✓ Coppice recently planted eucalyptus to encourage it to grow into a shrub

✓ Prune bush and shrub roses

✓ Cut back hard the coloured stems of dogwood and salix

✓ Renovate climbers by cutting them back hard

MARCH 2015

WEDNESDAY

25

THURSDAY

26

FRIDAY

27

SATURDAY

28

SUNDAY

29

MONDAY

30

TUESDAY

31

Your notes

WEATHER:

PLANTS IN BLOOM:

TO DO:

true or false?

The creator and founder of Cornwall's Eden Project (and also the driving force behind the Lost Gardens of Heligan), is a Dutch-born businessman whose name is the same when read forwards OR backwards!

(Answer at the bottom of page 59)

PLANT IT

Colour from summer bulbs

How to plant bulbs for summer

MANY SUMMER bulbs, corms or tubers can be planted now to create stunning displays in the garden.

The best time to get all of these in the ground is between late March and May. Frost-tender bulbs are best planted last, after the risk of frost has passed. This will vary on where you are in the country, but they can be started off in containers in the greenhouse and planted out later. Bulbs like to grow in free-draining soil with some well-rotted organic matter dug into it. If you are planting in heavy clay soil, mix in two buckets of coarse sand to every square metre of soil.

At this stage in spring, plant the bulbs quickly; leaving them in bags for too long will result in poor flowering.

Freesias are frost-tender; they can be planted in pots or in the ground, but only after the last frosts of spring. They are great for cut flowers. Lilies are generally hardy so can go in now

If planting in heavy clay soil, place a handful of sand under the bulbs to improve drainage

Six summer bulbs to grow

- **Freesia (right top):** These are tender corms, and they do well in pots. Plant the corms 1-2in (2.5-5cm) deep and 3-4in(7.5-9cm) apart

- **Tigridia:** If planting outside choose a south or west facing bed. Wait until the risk of frosts has passed to plant outdoors, or plant in containers in a greenhouse or coldframe. Plant 2in (5cm) deep and 6in (15cm) apart

- **Homeria:** These grow well in sandy soil. Plant 1-2in (2.5-5cm) deep in groups, or use as a 'filler'

- **Gladiolus (right bottom):** Plant in an open, sunny site for the best flowers until the end of May. Plant 3in (7.5cm) deep, and 8in (20cm) apart

- **Lily:** These bulbs appreciate leaf mould added to the planting hole to help keep their roots cool. Plant 6in (15cm) deep and 12in (30cm) apart

- **Dahlia:** For early flowering, start dahlias off in moist compost in boxes protected from frosts, and then plant out in May. If planting directly outdoors, do it after the last frost, at a depth of about 4-6in (10-15cm)

In containers

- **Choose a pot deep enough for the bulb to sit at its correct planting depth**
- Place broken pot 'crocks' at the bottom of the pots to aid drainage
- **Place a layer of multipurpose compost with added grit into the pot base**
- Generally, bulbs (and this dahlia tuber) should be set at three times their depth
- **Sit bulbs with their shoots upwards**
- Cover the bulbs with compost, and water them in. Apply a high potash feed when growth is seen

In the ground

- **Plant in groups for a stunning border display**
- As a rough guide, the planting hole should be double the size of the bulb
- **If planting bulbs for cut flowers, such as gladioli (pictured), dig a trench and plant in staggered rows**
- Always plant them nose or shoot upwards
- **Cover with soil and gently firm down with the back of a rake**
- Mark the area so you are aware of where they are planted, thus avoiding treading on and damaging young growth

Greenhouse tomatoes

How to succeed with toms in growing bags

IF YOU have a greenhouse – or a conservatory you don't mind filling with greenery – you can now plant tomatoes into growing bags. They should become nicely established and actively growing before plants destined for outdoor cultivation are even a few inches high!

Growing bags are so useful because they are convenient, self-contained and space-saving. Tomatoes are particularly suited to them. The compost within (unless the bag is labelled as being formulated specifically for leafy crops, potatoes, herbs or flowers) is generally tailored to fruiting plants, such as toms.

The main downside to bags is that they contain a limited amount of compost, meaning that they dry out relatively quickly compared to plants growing in the garden soil. However, there are several ways to prevent this happening.

First, you could grow just two plants per bag rather than the recommended three. Or you could stand the bag on its side (propped so it stays upright), which then gives a greater depth of soil for the roots to grow in. You can also set up an irrigation system to deliver a controlled amount of water throughout the day, so they do not dry out if you are away.

Alternatively, and this is often the favoured option, plant the young tomato plants in a bottomless flowerpot set on the surface of the growing bag compost. This gives a greater volume of compost for the roots to grow in and establish. It also results in less watering and feeding as the bags hold moisture better. See the next page to find out how to do it.

Tomatoes are some of the most popular of plants grown by home gardeners: 25 per sent of all garden owners grow them each year

FYI
Before planting your tomatoes shake the compost in the growing bag to loosen and get rid of any lumps

Step by step

Planting 'bottomless pot' tomatoes in growbags

1 With a sharp knife, cut a round hole in the bag. Most bags house three plants, but cropping can sometimes be better with just two.

2 For each plant, take a 7in (17.5cm) plastic pot and remove some of the base. Push this into the hole you have created in the bag.

3 Place multipurpose compost in the pot so that it merges with the compost in the bag, and then plant your tomato plant into it.

4 Insert a supporting cane into the pot (but don't damage the roots); tie the tomato plant to it, and finally water the plant in.

The feeding regime

To get the best crop of tomatoes you need to feed the plants properly – fail to feed and you'll fail to achieve any kind of a decent yield later in the year.

What many gardeners tend to do is feed their plants weekly with a weak solution of organic seaweed fertiliser – this is done from the time the seedlings have been potted up until the first flowers have set. At this point the weekly feed should be changed to a high-potash tomato fertiliser, such as Tomorite. In all cases, combining these feeds with watering means hardly any extra time and effort is required.

MOW IT

Spring jobs to improve lawns

Post-winter (and pre-summer) the grass needs attention

GIVING YOUR lawn a facelift at any time of year will not just improve it – it automatically makes the rest of the garden look tidy as well. But of course now that we are heading into early spring, this is the best time to tackle any bare patches, as well as overgrown edges, moss and weeds.

Weeds such as white clover, daisies and dandelions can rob the soil of essential nutrients, causing the grass to lose its vigour and growth.

Listed here are the major jobs that need to be done now. Spend a bit of time looking after your lawn now to get it back into tip top condition and you'll be ready for those sunny summer days when you can enjoy it to its full.

Keep the blades on your lawnmower high for the first few cuts

The first cut

Set the blades high on mowers, to just take off the tops of the grass. Keep the cut high for a few weeks, until the grass is producing strong growth. Mowing too short at this time of year will weaken the grass and encourage weeds and moss to grow through any gaps that appear.

BARE PATCHES

Bare patches in lawns can be repaired at this time of year. Cut out the damaged area with a spade or half-moon iron, lightly fork over the soil that's exposed, and replace with new turf cut to size.

To repair using seed, lightly fork over the patch, add a little multipurpose compost, thinly sprinkle grass seed on the top, then cover the area with a protective barrier (such as netting) to stop birds eating the seed. Water in, and water again in dry weather.

Weeds & moss

■ The best time to get rid of weeds and moss is in spring. It is a good idea to use combined weed/feed and mosskill products, so that the grass thickens up and prevents growth of unwanted plants. Lawn sand (*right*) is a moss killer. Apply in dry weather when the soil is moist. Follow instructions on the packet. When moss turns black, scarify the lawn. Dig out large weeds using a daisy grubber, or for a chemical option, use a selective lawn weedkiller.

Lawn edges

■ After the grass has been cut, trim the lawn edges for a neat finish. Winter rain causes movement and compression of soil, resulting in uneven growth and shape. Because of this, using edging shears may be difficult, so it is best to use a half-moon edging iron (*left*) to re-define the edges.

FYI
Areas of dry shade, such as under trees, become sparse very quickly. Over-seed yearly to maintain a dense sward

Slug and snail control in 2015

These pests are a problems for gardeners – every year

SLUGS ARE worse in wet years, and March is the time to get on top of the problem – as seedlings emerge and garden plants come back into leafy growth, slugs will be gearing up to feast on all that tender growth. And to make things worse, we're now under threat from an armada of Spanish 'killer' slugs thought to have come to the UK on imported salad leaves.

The new species reaches 5in (12.5cm) long, and as well as chomping on plants, will happily munch on dead animals, pet mess and even each other (so, every cloud...!). Entomologists at the John Innes Centre predict that millions of them will emerge in gardens and open spaces in the UK this year.

There are ways of keeping slugs at bay with minimal chemical use. It is now said that slugs tend to live within an area just 16ft (4.8m) in diameter. Knowing this, just a few traps are needed to cover a small garden. This news has changed many gardeners from being pellet scatterers, to the more considered users of traps. Whether you are an organic gardener or not, the controls here should fight off a slug attack.

There are many brands of slug killer available

Nematodes

These are microscopic eelworms that enter slugs and release a bacteria that stops the slugs from feeding. They then reproduce inside the slug and the next generation moves on in the search of more prey.

Once slug numbers dwindle the nematodes die back to natural levels. Nemaslug is widely available online for mail-ordering.

Call in the coppers!

Be prepared!

When slug pellets are used according to instructions (spread thinly!) pets and wildlife will not consume sufficient quantities to cause injury or death. In fact, pellets are deliberately made unattractive to all animals other than molluscs (blue is unattractive to birds), and include bittering agents and other repellents.

So don't feel you are a bad gardener if you want to scatter the pellets across planting beds to protect emerging growth (*above*) at the start of the season.

For season-long protection you will need to do this several times through the year, particularly after reworking and planting areas with seasonal bedding.

If scattering pellets does worry you, why not try a decorative pellet holder (there are a number of designs on the market). This will hide the pellets from view, as well as curious pets and young children. Similar to the Slug Bell (*left*) the pellets will last longer and fewer applications will be needed.

The science behind copper as a barrier is still unexplained. Some say slugs are given an electric shock, others say this a myth. The makers of slug rings have been using their products on the veg patch for a decade and claim a 95 per cent success rate in keeping slugs off the crops. The secret of success with barriers like this (and copper tape for use around pots), is to ensure there are no slugs trapped inside the barrier before it is put into place.

Slug pubs

These can be a yoghurt pot or jar, half filled with beer, milk or fruit juice, buried to near its rim amongst your plants. The slugs (and snails) can't resist a fermenting drink, and soon slip in and drown. Be warned – the contents can become slimy and unpleasant, so empty it regularly, or just put a few pellets in – a lot less messy. Cover the top to keep rain water out.

Natural methods

■ You will have fewer slug and snail problems if you actively encourage wildlife to your garden. Hedgehogs, frogs and toads, slow-worms, thrushes and other birds will home in on these molluscs as a favourite source of food. One toad can eat up to 100 slugs per night! Create little hidey-holes, and offer other food for these beneficial creatures. Also, cut an orange or grapefruit in half and eat the contents. Then place the empty half, white-side down, onto your garden soil. Over night slugs, and perhaps some snails too, will congregate underneath it. They can then be dispatched the following morning.

Masterclass

Caring for plug plants

Growing from plug plants is convenient and relatively cheap

Look after these young plants and they will reward you well in 2015

THERE ARE many reasons why people buy plug plants. For example, some plants are difficult to raise from seed at home, needing exact temperatures and light (which are easier to control in a nursery). Also, certain plant varieties are only available as young plants. And if a home-grown crop fails, plugs are a great way of quickly filling any gaps created.

However, plugs do still need some care to help them grow into the plants of our dreams. They have been raised in a controlled environment, of course, which means they are not used to outdoor spring temperatures (which can result in poor establishment if the plants are put out early).

It is important when buying plug plants to check them over. Look out for spindly growth, yellow wilting leaves, dry compost and signs of pests and diseases.

All plug plants should come with care information, and if mail-ordered plants arrive in a poor state, complain.

FYI
Plug plants will grow on quite happily on a sunny windowsill if you don't have a conservatory or greenhouse

Hardening off

■ Plug and bedding plants after potting on will need to be acclimatised to their new surroundings. Place them in a cold frame or greenhouse for a few days, or place them outdoors on warm days, protecting them from chilly spring nights, by covering in fleece or bringing them back indoors.

MARCH

S	M	T	W	T	F	S
1	2	3	4	5	6	7
8	9	10	11	12	13	14
15	16	17	18	19	20	21
22	23	24	25	26	27	28
29	30	31				

Clocks go forward

Start planting!

Plug plant sizes explained

MINI

ST'RD

LARGE

JUMBO

These are the best value plug plants, as they are very small. The seed has been germinated and has produced a root system, but is delivered before they need planting up. Ideally they should be potted on, straight away when you get them. Although some instructions say plant direct, they are too small and some will still need thinning out. Pot them on into either 3in (7.5cm) pots or into large module trays.

Standard size plugs, if ordered online will arrive in little plastic 'greenhouses'. Each section holding a plant will be lettered. It is best to write plant labels for each plug plant before removing it from the container, so they cannot get muddled up. Pot them up into 3in (7.5cm) to 3.5in (9cm) pots using multi-purpose compost.

These are grown to a size where they could be planted directly into their final place, but if a poor spring they will still need time to settle and develop more roots. Plant into 3.5in (9cm) pots.

These are well-developed plants with relatively large rootballs, needing a small period of adjustment to their new surroundings, before they are ready to be planted out.

Pinching out plug plants

■ Sometimes larger plug plants will put on vigorous growth once potted on, and may develop flower buds. It is best to pinch out young flower buds or any erratic growth seen until they are in their final position, so they can concentrate on producing roots.

Step by step ▸ Potting up mini plug plants

1 Fill a module tray with compost, and then water both the tray and plug plants; allow to drain. Dib holes in each module, using a dibber or pencil.

2 Turn to the plug tray, and push the end of the dibber or pencil into each hole in the bottom of each compartment, to push out the plug, without damaging it.

3 Pot up the plug, firm it in, water again and label the plants. Set them in a cold greenhouse or coldframe, or on a sunny windowsill. Water when dry.

TRUE OR FALSE FROM p49: **TRUE.** His man in question is Tim Smit *(pictured on p49)*.

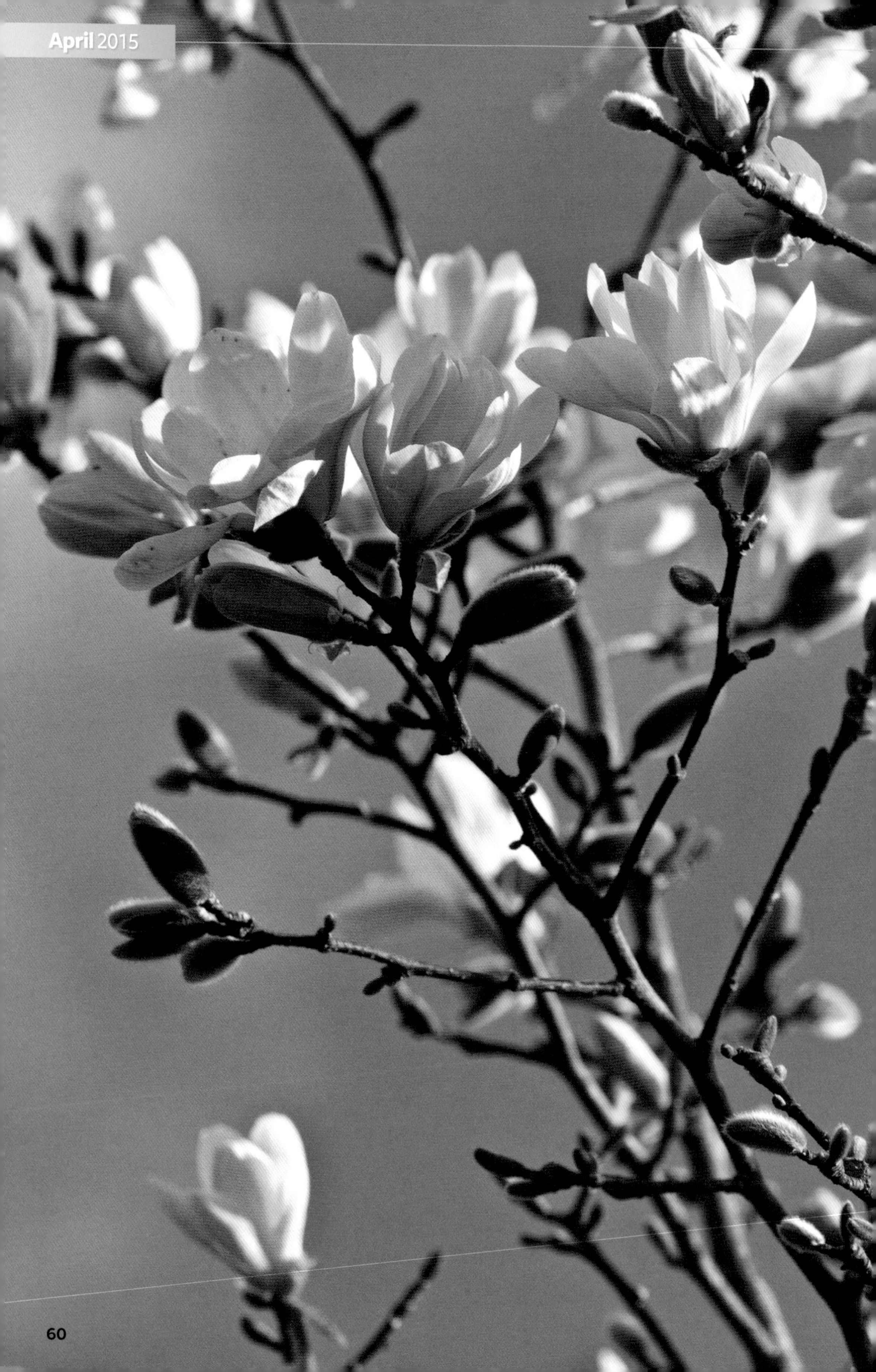

APRIL

Although the increasing warmth and sun, along with the rising soil and air temperatures, promote growth in the garden in April, everything can be brought to a halt by one night of frost. Spring frosts are always a major threat when the wind comes from a northerly direction, when the sky clears and the wind dies away at dusk, especially when the soil surface is dry. Horticultural fleeces, cloches, coldframes...these all come into their own at this stage in spring.

The dangerous years are those when both March and April have been very dry months, as this can mean that there is a serious risk of a frost in May.

April colour comes from crab apples, cherries (flowering and fruiting types), berberis, early brooms and clematis, and the young red growths of pieris.

◁ *Magnolias are magnificent in April. There are some that remain medium-size shrubs (such as Magnolia stellata), and others that reach 25ft (7.5m) garden trees, like this* Magnolia x loebneri

The garden in *April*

With more than 40 acres (16ha) of informal woodlands, walks and a walled garden, it's not surprising that visitors sometimes don't know where to start. The gardens have probably the largest private collection of plants in Wales. The Woodland Garden is full of rhododendrons, camellias and magnolias. The garden is also home to dozens of rare, endangered conifers from as far away as Taiwan and Australia, keeping species alive as their natural habitat declines. There are lots of exotic ferns and bamboos, too.

HOW TO GET THERE: The castle and garden is located two miles South of the A40. Follow the brown tourist signs to Picton Castle that are located on the A40 approx 3 miles East of Haverfordwest. Car parking is free. For more information, visit www.pictoncastle.co.uk.

OPENING TIMES: Open daily 10.30am – 5.00pm. Gardens may be closed in bad weather or in high wind.

Picton Castle & Gardens, Pembrokeshire SA62 4AS

5 top plants for April

1 *Berberis darwinii* is one of the brightest and most consistently good shrubs for spring.
2 If you have an acid soil, and can provide some dappled shade, try *Pieris formosa* var *forestii* 'Wakehurst'.
3 'Debbie' is a pink, large-flowered camellia from New Zealand, but is widely available in the UK.
4 *Ceanothus* 'Blue Mound' is one of the best of the Californian lilacs, and needs a sunny spot to grow well.
5 One of the flowering quinces – *Chaenomeles* 'Knaphill Scarlet'.

This month in
Gardening
history

■ *4 APR 1609*
Carolus Clusius (*below*) died. He was a pioneering botanist and influential 16th century gardener. He was the first to realise that viruses were the causes of colour breaks in tulips. He was born in 1526.

■ *6 APR, 1974*
Champion vegetable grower **Colin Bowcock** plants six potatoes in a specially prepared bed. Together they yield 2963lb (1344kg) five months later, a world record at the time.

■ *21 APR, 1637*
The thee-year 'Tulipomania' period ended in Holland, with the collapse of the tulip market. At its height, a single tulip bulb was sold for more than the price of a house in Amsterdam.

APRIL 2015

WEDNESDAY

1

THURSDAY

2

FRIDAY

3

SATURDAY

4

SUNDAY

5

MONDAY

6

TUESDAY

7

WEDNESDAY

8

AT A GLANCE
JOBS TO DO THIS MONTH

 GENERAL TASKS

- Slugs and other pests will start to come in force this month – keep on top of them.
- Apply a light dressing of fertiliser such as blood, fish and bone around the borders.
- Keep borders ticking over – fork over, weed and hoe.

 LAWNS

- Feed grass (in the south); re-seed bare patches and treat moss and weeds.
- Mow lawns once a fortnight (*right*); keep up with edging.
- Sow grass seed for a new lawn if you can't wait until autumn.

 TREES, SHRUBS AND CLIMBERS

- Continue to plant or move evergreens.
- Continue to plant container-grown woody plants.
- Tie-in climbing roses (*below*), wall-trained shrubs and newly planted climbers.

APRIL 2015

THURSDAY

9

FRIDAY

10

SATURDAY

11

SUNDAY

12

MONDAY

13

TUESDAY

14

WEDNESDAY

15

THURSDAY

16

Use a coldframe to start hardening off plants

your notes

WEATHER:

PLANTS IN BLOOM:

TO DO:

APRIL 2015

FRIDAY

17

SATURDAY

18

SUNDAY

19

MONDAY

20

TUESDAY

21

WEDNESDAY

22

THURSDAY

23

FRIDAY

24

AT A GLANCE
JOBS TO DO THIS MONTH

FLOWERS

- [ ] Keep planting and dividing perennials.
- [ ] Deadhead daffodil flowers (*right*).
- [ ] Plant summer bulbs and *Anemone* de Caen in borders or containers.
- [ ] Sow hardy annuals direct (in the north).
- [ ] Sow sweet peas direct (in the south).

IN THE GREENHOUSE

- [ ] Start hardening off summer bedding during the day.
- [ ] Pot up rooted cuttings from last year.
- [ ] Pot on begonias.
- [ ] Buy and pot up plug plants.
- [ ] Plant up a hanging basket and keep it under protection.

CONTAINERS AND PATIOS

- [ ] Remove winter protection from pots (*right*).
- [ ] Plant spring bedding in containers.

WHAT TO PRUNE

- ✓ Forsythia
- ✓ Chaenomeles
- ✓ Lavender
- ✓ Sambucus and cotinus (for foliage)
- ✓ Hydrangea
- ✓ Winter jasmine

APRIL 2015

SATURDAY

25

SUNDAY

26

MONDAY

27

TUESDAY

28

WEDNESDAY

29

THURSDAY

30

Your notes

WEATHER:

PLANTS IN BLOOM:

TO DO:

true or false?

The centre of our galaxy tastes like blackcurrants!

(Answer at the bottom of page 75)

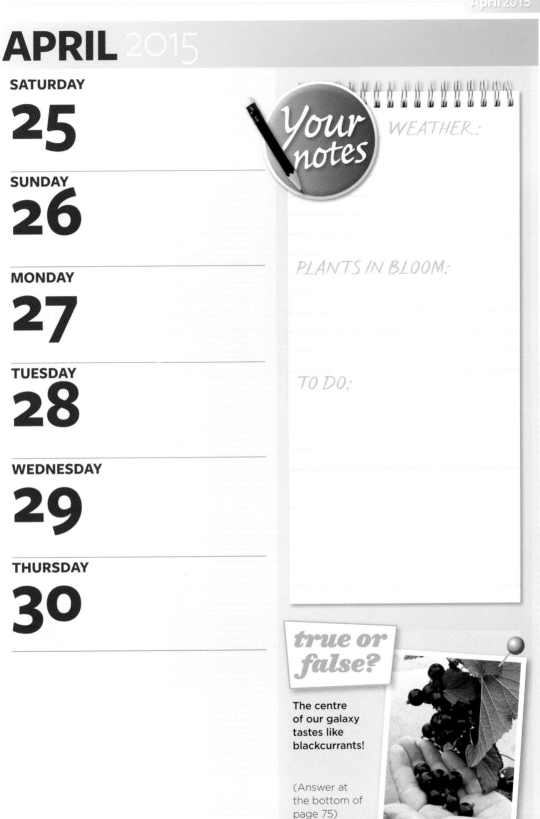

PLANT IT

Containers for spring

FYI
The best site for a hanging basket is partly sunny during the day, and protected from strong winds

Tips on creating that perfect spring container

I F YOU did not manage to plant up any spring baskets or containers before winter set in, and you've suddenly woken up to the fact that spring is here, it's not too late to give yourself some instant colour – even to the point of giving your garden or house front a special Easter theme!

There are places all around the garden for containers. Wherever you desire a compact splash of colour there is a type of container, and place for it, to fit the bill.

Patios, decks and balconies are all barren without a few pots of seasonal plants. And there is no such thing as a wall that cannot be enhanced by a couple of baskets or wall-pots to break up its plain-ness.

This is also your perfect opportunity to plant up something quirky (*see right*).

There are many types of annual and biennial flower, as well as smaller perennial plants, in bud or in full colour, available now from garden centres. These can be chosen to give instant colour, and will continue to bloom up until the start of summer.

Pots, urns, tubs, vases, windowboxes, hanging baskets…whatever your choice of container, there will be something for you.

Hanging baskets, particularly, can make a difference to a garden this early in spring. It is estimated that about a third of gardens have baskets of some kind, so let's see if we can raise this figure!

And by buying a few plants for instant colour from the garden centre, you won't miss out on a colourful garden this Easter on 5 April.

A little creativity on your part now, can transform your garden, patio or even balcony, in time for Easter

Cute containers

There is a huge interest in the unusual, the weird and the whacky! It is worth shopping around in your area…or to visit car boot sales or local junk shops, to see what containers are available (or even what can be used as a container, or converted into such).

As long as it can support soil and allow for drainage, you can use almost anything.

In recent years we've even seen items of lined clothing (bras, pants, trousers, etc) being used to contain plants.

Creating your own planters not only provides an opportunity for a fun project, but it also helps the environment by recycling objects that might otherwise wind up in a landfill.

Step by step ▶ How to make an Easter hanging basket

1 This is using one of the artificial grass basket liners available. It is easy to fit into any traditional and normal-sized basket. Once in, start to cover the base of the liner with multipurpose compost.

2 Place some dwarf narcissus, bought in a pot and already sprouting, into the centre of the basket. The shoots are not high yet, but when in flower the blooms will be heads above the surrounding plants.

3 Next to go in are some coloured hybrid primroses. There are so many colours to choose from – so you can choose to suit your scheme. Three, planted equidistantly around the narcissus, will look good.

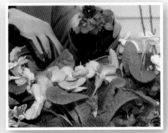

4 A basket always looks more pleasing if there is an element of verticality to it. Right now one or two variegated trailing ivies can provide this extra dimension. Your choice of trailing plants for summer baskets is so much greater, however.

5 The last plants to go into this spring basket are several deep blue violas, both as gap fillers in the top, and as plants to set at regular intervals along the side of the basket. Yellow and blue, incidentally, are typical spring colours.

6 Hang your basket to a purpose-made bracket. It is hugely important for this bracket to be securely fixed to the wall (or upright post, as here). The final stage is to water your plants, to allow them to establish.

7 best 'instant' container plants to last

▨ **Double bedding daisy (*Bellis perennis, right*)** – there are red, pink and white varieties, all with yellow centres

▨ **Brompton stock (*Matthiola incana*)** – delicious scent to keep near to doorways and entrances

▨ **Forget-me-not (*Myosotis alpestris*)** – good for underplanting taller subjects

▨ **Heuchera** – an evergreen perennial with year-round leaves in a wide variety of colours

▨ **Primroses** – modern hybrids come in every colour except bright green and black

▨ **Trailing ivies** – in variegated form, these are perfect for trailing down from hanging baskets and the sides of patio pots

▨ **Viola** – spring violas and pansies will flower into summer and often way beyond, and in a huge range of colours

Growing strawberries

STRAWBERRIES

Some simple steps to planting and growing delicious strawberries

S TRAWBERRIES ARE one of the most popular fruits to grow, and April is a great time to get them started. There are three main types: alpine (small in size), summer fruiting, and ever-bearers that produce fruit through summer and early autumn.

If possible, grow a few of each for a regular supply of fruit over the summer and into early autumn.

Strawberries can either be grown from seed, or bought as cold-stored runners (generally available from April until August), or open-ground runners (dug up and sent out between August and April). These are available from many of the major seed catalogues, or a specialist fruit supplier such as Ken Muir. Young plants grown in pots are widely available from garden centres.

To prepare a planting site outdoors, dig well-rotted organic garden compost or manure into the soil a few weeks before planting.

If you choose to grow strawberries from seed, you'll have to wait a little longer for fruits, but the up-side is the number of plants you will be able to grow at little cost.

FYI
Strawberry plants will produce less fruit as they get older. Replace them every five years to improve yield

Established strawberry plants need a tidy up, a feed high in potash to increase their fruit yields, and a mulch with some fresh compost

Strawberry black eye

■ At this time of year the main problem with early varieties is a condition called 'strawberry black eye'. The parts of the flower that produce the fruit become black due to frost damage, resulting in no fruit.

Protect early flowers from frost by covering with fleece or a cloche. Avoid planting early strawberries in exposed areas.

PLANTING COLD STORED STRAWBERRY RUNNERS

- **If planting strawberry runners directly into the ground, spacing should be about 18in (45cm) with the rows 30in (75cm) apart to allow for growth**

- When you unwrap the runners, remove dead foliage and soak the roots in water or a weak seaweed solution extract, for half an hour before planting

- **Dig a hole with a trowel big enough to spread the roots out, making sure the crown of the plant will be just showing on the top of the soil**

- Backfill the hole, firming down as you go. Once full, firm down around the plant crown

- **Water the plants in and do not let them dry out**

Six strawberry varieties to try

1. **'Florence'** (above)
2. 'Honeoye'
3. **'Marshmello'**
4. 'Cambridge'
5. **'Elsanta'**
6. 'Mignonette' (Alpine)

Growing in containers

Strawberries do well in pots, baskets or growing bags. They do need adequate space to grow – too many plants crammed in a pot will result in fewer fruits. For a 12in (30cm) pot or basket, use three strawberry plants. Use good potting compost enriched with well rotted manure. Check the compost daily, and keep watered so they do not dry out.

Established plants

If you already have strawberries in your garden, give them some attention now. Remove brown and dead leaves and any runners that have rooted over winter, which are not needed. If keeping some, cut the stem from the parent plant (*right*) to separate them. Add a layer of well-rotted manure or compost mulch to enrich the soil.

GROW IT

Early colour from camellias

A look at the essentials for getting some instant colour with camellias

FYI
Avoid growing camellias where they get early morning sun, as this can cause frosted blooms to drop early

WHO DOESN'T adore a gorgeous camellia when it's in full flower during the warming spring months? March and April are the key months for camellia blooms, although there are some that flower earlier and others that flower later than this. And right now, garden centres are full of them!

Now is a good time to buy a camellia, as you can see the flowers on the plant you're buying; even if the label is wrong (which does happen from time to time) you will not be disappointed if you buy the variety with the flower you like!

Don't forget, too, that camellias are acid-loving plants. So, if you have an acidic soil, then your garden will be lacking if it doesn't have a camellia in it. If your soil is chalky, then your garden will be lacking if it doesn't have a camellia in a pot of ericaceous compost. So either way, there is no reason not to have one!

Buying a flowering camellia now will mean that you are assured of the flower colour of your choice – and it'll brighten up your garden instantly

The colourful choice

■ 'Black Magic' is a rich, soft red camellia with slightly hidden yellow stamens. It also has curious holly-like leaves, produced on a fast growing, bushy plant.

Growing tips!

1. **The first thing to do when getting a camellia home is to tidy up the pot base. Remove weeds, moss and algae. It can also help to add an inch or two of ericaceous compost as a topdressing to help the plant in its new home.**

2. Camellias, as with most shrubs, do not like to have their roots languishing in over-wet compost. So stand the container on 'pot feet', to improve drainage. This will also prevent ants from invading the compost within the pot.

- **'Volunteer'** is a relatively recent introduction. This early flowering camellia has huge wine coloured, peony-like flowers with white markings to the petal edge.

3. Feed your plant – whether it's in a pot or in the ground. Being acid-loving plants, it is important to make sure that camellias are fed with an ericaceous feed, and there are several available from garden centres.

4. **During the late spring and summer, next year's flower buds will be forming. At this crucial time you must not allow your plants to dry out; this is particularly important with those growing in pots**

- **'Strawberry Parfait'** has large, semi-double or loose peony-like flowers with rose pink petals overlaid with crimson stripes. Bushes are upright, dense and moderately vigorous.

- **'Elegant Beauty'** is a later-flowering hybrid, producing free-flowering deep rose pink anemone-like blooms. Arching growth makes it ideal for training against a wall. It has bronze young foliage.

Masterclass

April

Alpine planters

Create a stunning display of flowers using alpines

ALPINES ARE small plants that look great in gravel beds, rockeries, walls, and of course containers. They are a family of plants that grow naturally in high mountainous areas, above a 'tree line' (the highest point trees will grow). This exposes them to a wide range of temperatures, poor soils and drying winds, hence why they are slow growing and small. They are best sited in an open, sunny position, but some will tolerate light shade.

If given the right conditions, alpines grow very well in the UK; though their roots can rot if planted in waterlogged soil. They need a very free draining soil to avoid this; in containers this is achieved by mixing in horticultural grit with a John Innes No2 or equivalent compost.

Alpines tend to be matt-forming, with delicate flowers and leaves, so are best viewed close up and usually planted in sinks or troughs (see below for guidance on hot to plant one up), as

Creating an alpine sink is not difficult

this allows for their beauty to be clearly seen. Have a go at planting a trough, to create a stunning display in an area of your garden.

Step by step — How to plant up an alpine trough

1 Place the trough where it is to be displayed, away from over-hanging branches and where water can't drip on to it. Place a layer of crocks in the bottom of the trough to aid drainage.

2 Fill with a mix of John Innes No.2 or equivalent with 50 per cent horticultural grit, leaving a gap of 5in (12.5cm) below the rim of the container. Firm down the compost.

3 Arranging the plants before planting. Place stones in the trough for added interest and for the roots to grow underneath . Set trailing plants near the edges.

Alpine colander

For a budget way of planting alpines, use an old colander. These are easily picked up in junk shops and at car boot sales.

- **Place some sphagnum moss in the bottom and around the sides**
- Half fill up with JI No.2 compost mixed with horticultural grit
- **Plant the alpines and fill with more mixed compost around them**
- Decorate the top with stone chippings or grit and water in

Containers

If using a stone trough or 'butler's sink' to plant alpines in, take into account where it's positioned. Because of its weight, it will be very difficult to move once planted up. You can buy alpine troughs made from lightweight polymer resin, which makes them much easier to transport.

Ensure there is at least one drainage hole in whatever type of container you use. It is a good idea to raise the container up from the ground using pot feet or bricks to allow for surplus water to drain quickly.

FYI
Use rocks in the display of alpines, as they more easily help to keep the plant roots cool

4 Start planting from one corner of the trough, and work your towards the opposite diagonal one. Firm the soil around the plants and then water them in.

5 Add a layer of grit or small stone chippings in a colour of your choice over the surface of the soil to help with drainage, and for a decorative finish.

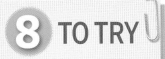

8 TO TRY

There is an enormous variety of alpine plants available from garden centres and specialist nurseries; here are a few of the favourites

- ***Saxifraga arendsii* 'Neon Rose'** (*below*)

- *Primula capitata* ssp. *mooreana*
- ***Saxifraga* 'Lutea'**
- *Lithodora diffusa* 'Heavenly Blue'
- ***Aubrieta* x *hybrida* 'Audrey Blue'**
- *Arabis* 'Snowcap'
- ***Artemisia schmidtiana* 'Nana'**
- *Euphorbia myrsinites*

APRIL calendar — 6 circled, Bank Holiday

MAY

Once spring has really arrived to stay, and summer is not far away, the essential ingredients for good growth are energy from the sun, plant food from soil nutrients and, most of all, soil moisture available to the roots, without which the rest are useless. There are often dry spells in May, so to make good any deficit, gardens need watering if it is dry. It has been estimated that, on average, around now a garden will use 1in (2.5cm) of water – that is, 4½gal (24litres) of water – every 10 days.

It is the vegetable garden that profits most from skilful maintenance of soil moisture regimes; heavy crops cannot be grown on a dry soil.

Hawthorns, laburnums, mountain ash, ceanothus, tree peonies, potentillas, pyracanthas, and of course rhododendrons and azaleas, are all providing important colour now. This is also the best month for tulips.

Tulip 'Apricot Beauty' works brilliantly with many spring-flowering herbaceous plants, including hellebores, Solomon's seal and blue forget-me-nots. Tulips need to be planted late in October and November

The garden in *May*

Compton Acres was built in 1924 and is a wonderful example of the UK's historic and idiosyncratic gardens. It is 10 acres (4ha), and is of late Victorian mixed style design with seven distinct gardens to wander around and enjoy, including the famous Italian and Japanese Gardens. There is a magnificent collection of more than 3000 species of trees, shrubs, herbaceous plants and bulbs.

HOW TO GET THERE: The garden is near to Sandbanks, Poole, and is signposted from the A338 and A35. Follow the brown and white tourist signs. Car parking is free. For details of public transport, visit www.comptonacres.co.uk and follow the links.

OPENING TIMES: Open every day except Christmas Day and Boxing Day. Times: Good Friday – 31 October 10-6pm (last entry 5pm, shops close 5pm); from 1 November 10-4pm (last entry 3pm; ticket Office closes at 3pm, other shops close 5pm).

Compton Acres, Poole, Dorset BH13 7ES

5 top plants for May

1 *Hyacinthoides non-scriptus* – the English bluebell – is a familiar sight in spring.
2 *Kalmia latifolia* is an acid-loving woodland shrub at its best in late spring.
3 Of all the garden-worthy rhododendrons, the pink 'Doc' is one of the best.
4 Oenothera – the evening primrose – has bright yellow flowers.
5 *Penstemon* 'Blue Springs' is a delightful perennial (if slightly tender) with flowers of bright royal blue.

This month in *Gardening* history

2 MAY 1949
Alan Titchmarsh, gardening writer and presenter – and now a TV celebrity – was born, near Ilkley Moor in Yorkshire.

3 MAY, 1884
The first ever edition of *Amateur Gardening* (*above*) appeared on bookstands across Victorian Britain. It has since endured two World Wars and numerous conflicts and financial crises – and is still the best-loved gardening magazine around today.

18 MAY, 1830
Inventor **Edwin Budding** signed an agreement with John Ferrabee of the Phoenix Iron Works, Stroud, for the manufacture of the first commercially available lawnmower.

MAY

FRIDAY

1

SATURDAY

2

SUNDAY

3

MONDAY

4

TUESDAY

5

WEDNESDAY

6

THURSDAY

7

FRIDAY

8

AT A GLANCE
JOBS TO DO THIS MONTH

GENERAL TASKS

☐ Continue to hoe the soil to keep weed seedlings down.

☐ Keep an eye out for pests and diseases – and act quickly if you see any.

☐ Set beer traps for slugs.

PONDS

☐ Remove excess pondweed, which clogs water (*right*).

☐ Feed fish regularly.

☐ Plant water lilies.

LAWNS

☐ Mow the lawn weekly.

☐ Use lawn clippings to mulch borders.

☐ Feed the lawn in cold regions.

TREES, SHRUBS AND CLIMBERS

☐ Tie-in climbers.

☐ Trim evergreen hedging.

☐ Water newly planted trees and shrubs.

MAY

SATURDAY

9

SUNDAY

10

MONDAY

11

TUESDAY

12

WEDNESDAY

13

THURSDAY

14

FRIDAY

15

SATURDAY

16

Watch out for, and destroy, scarlet lily beetles

Your notes

WEATHER:

PLANTS IN BLOOM:

TO DO:

MAY

SUNDAY
17

MONDAY
18

TUESDAY
19

WEDNESDAY
20

THURSDAY
21

FRIDAY
22

SATURDAY
23

SUNDAY
24

AT A GLANCE
JOBS TO DO THIS MONTH

FLOWERS

- [ ] Plant out sweet pea plants.
- [ ] Thin hardy annual seedlings.
- [ ] Cut back pulmonarias and aubrieta.
- [ ] Feed spring-flowering bulbs.
- [ ] Clear out spring bedding.
- [ ] Plant out tender bedding and dahlias.
- [ ] Sow seed of perennials.

CONTAINERS AND PATIOS

- [ ] Keep on top of watering pots and hanging baskets.
- [ ] Plant up summer containers.

IN THE GREENHOUSE

- [ ] Move conservatory plants outdoors.
- [ ] Take cuttings from tender geraniums and fuchsias between now and autumn.
- [ ] Shade glass (*right*) and check temperatures
- [ ] Bring out earlier-planted hanging baskets, or plant one up.

WHAT TO PRUNE

- ✓ **Give early-flowering clematis a light prune if needed**
- ✓ *Kerria japonica*
- ✓ *Spiraea 'Arguta'*
- ✓ **Forsythia**
- ✓ *Ribes sanguineum*

MAY

MONDAY

25

TUESDAY

26

WEDNESDAY

27

THURSDAY

28

FRIDAY

29

SATURDAY

30

SUNDAY

31

Your notes

WEATHER:

PLANTS IN BLOOM:

TO DO:

true or false?

Sports broadcaster Bob Wilson, a former Arsenal and Scotland goalkeeper, has the middle name of Daisy.

(Answer at the bottom of page 91)

GROW IT

Hydrangeas for summer

Plant hydrangeas to add some colour to your summer garden

MOPHEAD HYDRANGEAS divide us gardeners – you either love 'em or hate 'em! If the pink or blue pompoms of *H. macrophylla* are just too brash for your liking, dig a little deeper and you'll find a range of varieties more subtle and classier for summer use.

Lacecap types, *H. macrophylla nomilis*, have a looser, flatter flower head compared to the mopheads. This shape can also be found on the low growing Japanese mountain hydrangea, *H. serrata*.

H. paniculata offers pure white conical flowers at least 8in (20cm) long. Varieties like 'Limelight' start off green and fade to pink towards autumn, while 'Pink Diamonds' starts creamy-white, turning pink/red later in the season.

All hydrangeas offer good autumn leaf colour, but for year-round foliage impact try the oak leaf variety, *H. quercifolia*. And don't forget climbing *H. anomala* and *H. seemanii* for covering walls, trellis, fencing etc.

All hydrangeas perform best in semi-shade, but *H. paniculata* will take full sun if kept moist

FYI
If mopheads turn blue your soil is acidic; pink and it is an alkaline soil; mauve and it's neutral

at the roots through summer.

If you're worried about a basic lack of colour until the flowers open, grow hydrangeas with rhododendrons. The hydrangea will take over in early summer as its flower heads emerge and provide a mass of colour for mid-summer. And don't forget that dried hydrangea heads can be left on the plants for winter interest, too.

Mophead hydrangea

Lacecap hydrangea

PLANTING IN THE GROUND

ADD PLENTY of organic matter (compost or rotted manure) to the soil and a bit of bonemeal to the planting hole (*inset*) and no further feeding should be needed, unless you work on very light sandy soil.

Here, a spring topdressing of fish, blood and bone will be of benefit. On richer soils, feeding can lead to too much leafy growth at the expense of flowers, so only feed if plants develop yellowish leaves.

Step by step — Planting in containers

1 Water the plant in its pot. While draining make a 50/50 mix of multipurpose compost and John Innes No.3. Add gravel to the bottom of your container to help drainage, and part fill.

2 Set the rootball, teasing out dense roots by scratching the surface. Fill around the roots with the compost mix, firming down until the rootball is just covered. Water in and mulch.

3 To tidy, prune stems back to strong buds, aiming to slightly dome the canopy. Remove weak side shoots low down and in the centre, to keep an open habit for good air circulation.

GROW IT

Making the most of herbs

Herbs are very versatile – they look great in baskets, containers and, of course, mixed borders

HERBS HAVE been grown in this country for thousands of years; they were even used as currency! Now our economic climate is not yet that bad to grow them for that purpose, but they are ideal plants to use all around the garden, for colour, foliage, smell and of course to eat.

Herbs can be annual, biennial and perennial, many come from the Mediterranean so prefer to grow in a sunny position with well-drained soil. Also, take into account when choosing a site, that it is easily accessible for you to look after and pick them. They grow well in containers and can be sited near the kitchen door for use. Hardy annual herbs and perennial herbs can be sown or planted outside in the ground now.

If planting in containers, have one pot with hardy varieties in it, the other with the tender annuals such as basil. Herbs prefer a pot that allows them to grow deep roots, such as a tomato pot. Established plants can also be propagated for extra stock in spring, read on for tips on how to do this.

FYI
Sow dill directly outdoors to add foliage with texture to mixed flower borders

Never be without a few herbs to use in the kitchen

Planting in the ground

Harden off young herb plants before planting out in a weed free area. Gently push the plant out of its pot, handle them by their leaves or rootball not their stems as these can be easily damaged. Plant them into a hole, so the top of their rootball is just below the surface. Firm in and water. Keep watering, especially in dry spells until they are established.

Step by step ▶ Planting in containers

1 Choose a pot that is deep enough for the herbs to put on roots – a tomato pot is best. Add multi-purpose compost with added grit into the bottom until two thirds up

2 Position the herbs in the pot to see how they look, and whether they look good next to each other or separated by others. Plant in odd numbers if possible.

3 Firm the herbs in position, using your fingers, and fill around them with more of the same compost. Label to distinguish between the plants, and water in.

Dividing

Chives, marjoram, mint, oregano and thyme can all be divided in spring, giving them plenty of time to establish before the autumn.

■ Lift the plants carefully, with a garden fork

■ If the plants are small, gently pull them apart with your fingers, ensuring there are plenty of roots on each section

■ Bigger plants can be divided by simply cutting through the middle using a clean knife (**pictured**)

■ With larger herbs, insert two garden forks back-to-back and prise apart

■ Plant or pot on the herbs immediately and water well

Sowing hardy herbs

Many herbs can be grown successfully from seed. In early spring sow the hardy herbs, for example tarragon, chives, coriander and mint. Later, when the weather is warmer, sow tender herbs such as basil.

■ Fill either pots or module trays with seed compost

■ Tap to settle the compost, water and allow to drain

■ Sprinkle the seed thinly and evenly on the top of the compost

■ Some herbs need a fine layer of sieved compost over them; some need more light to germinate, check the instructions on the seed packet

■ If warm enough, place in a coldframe or unheated greenhouse

■ Prick out the seedlings individually when true leaves have formed

GROW IT

Tender vegetables

Warm-loving veg can be started now inside – or outside in mild areas

Many who grow veg from seed will have been sowing hardy types outside since March, and even earlier with heat under cover. But now is the time to sow those frost-tender types (such as runner beans, sweetcorn and courgettes).

If the weather is still cold where you are, you will need to exercise caution by sowing in the protected environment of a greenhouse or coldframe, for planting out the seedlings later.

On the other hand if you live in a warm part, or you have a sheltered garden that rarely gets frosted, then you could risk a direct sowing outside from now. But you would still be advised to cover the rows with cloches or fleece until you know for a fact that frosts are finished!

If you think your garden might get more frosts this spring, play safe and sow tender veg under cover in a propagator or on a warm windowsill

And if the weather's warm...

Many grow sweetcorn and runner beans (*right*) by sowing directly outside. This is best done at the end of May, so that by the time green shoots are showing, frosts are well past. However, if soil is warm and the garden does not tend to get frosted in May, you can sow outside earlier in the month.

Other frost-tender vegetables to sow now

Although fruiting veg such as aubergines, tomatoes and peppers should have been started a few weeks back, you could still make a late sowing now. Others to sow now include:

- Vegetable marrow
- Sweet melon – only really successful in the UK as a greenhouse or frame crop
- Pumpkin and winter squashes
- Gherkins – a good outdoor crop
- Tomatillo – too big for greenhouses, but only does well outside in a hot summer
- Okra – only successful in greenhouses
- Cucumbers – there are greenhouse varieties and outdoor, or ridge, varieties (*pictured*), so make sure you choose the right variety for your situation

Courgettes, sweetcorn and runner beans under cover

COURGETTES

Sow in a greenhouse now for planting out under cloches or frames in late spring. Sow seeds on their sides (this helps germination); they'll also need a minimum of 13°C (56°F) to germinate successfully.

SWEETCORN

Sow two seeds per small coir pots filled with multipurpose compost. Keep at 20-27°C (68-80°F). Pinch out weakest seedling in each pot. From early June, plant out the seedlings in blocks (to assist wind pollination).

RUNNER BEANS

The hardiest of these three, runners are still damaged if frost occurs. The temperature for germination needs to be 12°C (54°F) or more. Sow 2in (5cm) deep in pots for planting out in a couple of weeks.

Masterclass

May

Keep weeds at bay!

Keep your garden weed-free this season with our timely maintenance tips

WHY IS it, that no matter how well we plant our gardens, it's always the weeds amongst our prized specimens that catch the eye. Friends and family won't likely notice the odd weed among your flower displays, but when you spend so much time and effort controlling the appearance of your own plot, you can't help but zone in on the weeds that escaped your attention.

Whether your garden is weed free and you want to keep it that way, or you've been lax on controlling them and have some weeding to do, the tips here should keep you on track.

Don't let weeds take over!

Hoe, hoe, hoe!

■ Regular hoeing or cultivation of garden soil is the best way to prevent weeds taking hold. Scratch over the soil weekly with a hoe or clawed hand cultivator and it's an easy job – but watch out for emerging perennial flowers. The soil never has time to compact, and any weeds that sprout over the week are easily sliced through or lifted to wither on the surface.

Do it less frequently and soil is harder to work, and annual weeds may have time to flower and set seed.

MAY

S	M	T	W	T	F	S
		Early May holiday			1	2
3	4	5	6	7	8	9
10	11	12	13	14	15	16
17	18	19	20	21	22	23
24	25	26	27	28	29	30
31						

Spring Bank Holiday

Patios and paving

Allow weeds to mature in the joins between patio slabs or block paving and it can be a real problem to remove them by hand. With no room to dig out tap roots, perennial weeds will likely return soon after pulling off or scraping away top growth.

Over time, regular removal of the re-growth will weaken the plant, eventually killing it, but if you don't mind using chemicals, the fastest route to a weed-free patio or path is to reach for a systemic weedkiller. These are absorbed by the plants and carried down to the roots to prevent any re-growth occurring. Apply these on a dry day, when there is no wind to blow spray on to plants or into neighbour's plots. One spray

usually does the job but a second may be needed.

Regular attention to hard surfaces will prevent the need for chemical sprays. The Burgon & Ball 'Compact' Miracle Block Paving Brush (*right*) is impressive with how easily the rows of wire bristles scrape away moss and young weed seedlings. Established weeds that have slipped notice until now can be easily prised out with the weeding knife blade attached to the tool.

TIPS FOR SUCCESS

- ✓ Hoe frequently, even when weeds are not visible
- ✓ Use long- or short-handled patio weeders (pictured)
- ✓ Kill weeds before they flower

FYI
Don't let a dandelion flower and then set seed. One seed head can produce 200 seeds that are all highly viable

Beds and borders

■ Aim to dig out weeds growing in border soils (pic) unless you're faced with persistent weeds that re-grow from bits of root left in the ground (ground elder, bindweed and couch grass spring to mind) .

Digging is eco-friendly, cheaper, and it removes the risk of damaging other plants with accidental spray drift. I tried for two years to rid a garden of couch grass this way, but it kept returning. The only way to control it was by spraying.

Heavy clay soils also make it difficult to dig out weeds without leaving roots in the ground, and again, sprays may be needed for total control. But if soils are easily workable it should be possible to lift even the longest tap roots of dandelion from the soil with a bit of careful digging.

TRUE OR FALSE FROM p83: **FALSE**. His middle name is actually Primrose, originating from a Scottish tradition of giving one's mother's maiden name as a middle name.

JUNE

The June garden is for enjoyment and entertainment – garden parties and barbecues start now in earnest. But remember that although June may have the longest days, and often brings the most sunshine, it is rarely the warmest month of the summer. It can, however, be dry, and then the watering problems of May become even more serious.

A favourite way to reduce the evaporative loss of moisture from open soil is by mulching. And a mulch also better allows the entry of water into the soil during a heavy rain – it prevents the soil becoming capped by a rapid drying out of the surface.

In June there is a wealth of colour to be had from flowering plants, including abelia, *Buddleja globosa*, cistus, deutzia, escallonia, helianthemum, peony, potentilla, jasmine and wisteria.

◁ *Think of June, and you think of sunshine, Wimbledon tennis – and strawberries! This is the variety 'Delician'*

The garden in *June*

A lush, tropical oasis perched on a peninsula at the edge of Loch Ewe amid the rugged landscape of Wester Ross. The garden – one of Scotland's most popular botanical attractions – was created out of bare rock and a few scrub willows in 1862, but is now full of colourful, exotic plants from around the world. Highlights include the most northerly planting of rare Wollemi pines, Himalayan blue poppies, olearia from New Zealand, Tasmanian eucalypts, and rhododendrons from China, Nepal and the Indian subcontinent.

HOW TO GET THERE: From Inverness, take the A835 then the A832. The journey, through some stunning Highland scenery, takes around 90 mins. For details of public transport, visit www.nts.org.uk, go to the Plan A Visit panel, and choose from the drop-down links.

OPENING TIMES: Open daily from April to October. From 1-30 Apr 10am-5pm. From 1-31 May 10am-5.30pm. From 1 Jun-31 Aug 9.30am-6pm. From 1-30Sept 10am-5pm. From 1-31 Oct 10am-4pm.

Inverewe,
Ross-shire
IV22 2LG

5 top plants
for June

This month in *Gardening* history

1 Ornamental onions are favourite flowers in late spring – this is *Allium* 'Globemaster'.
2 Clematises are perfect for climbing trellises and growing through trees – this is 'Ruby Glow'.
3 Fab foliage is to be had from hostas (this is 'Patriot'); watch for slugs.
4 One of the best of the blue flowers in the garden is from the annual climber *Ipomoea* 'Heavenly Blue'.
5 Foxgloves (*Digitalis purpurea*) in late spring/early summer.

■ *4 JUNE 1868*
Nathaniel Bagshaw Ward died. A London doctor, he was the inventor of the Wardian Case (*above*), a glass-sided case used to transport plants across the globe.

■ *12 JUNE, 1914*
John Seymour, prolific early author in the self-sufficiency movement, was born. His seminal book, *Self Sufficiency*, was published in 1970. He died in 2004.

■ *15 JUNE, 1621*
The first greenhouse in Britain was erected, in Oxford, in preparation for a predicted severe winter. It had no heating so a gardener had to wheel round a charcoal fire to keep the temperature up.

JUNE 2015

MONDAY

1

TUESDAY

2

WEDNESDAY

3

THURSDAY

4

FRIDAY

5

SATURDAY

6

SUNDAY

7

MONDAY

8

AT A GLANCE
JOBS TO DO THIS MONTH

GENERAL TASKS

- [ ] Mow and tend lawns.
- [ ] Apply spot treatments to weeds (*right*).
- [ ] Thin excessive growth of aquatic plants.
- [ ] Add tender pond plants.

TREES, SHRUBS AND CLIMBERS

- [ ] Clip box topiary.
- [ ] Deadhead camellias and rhododendrons.
- [ ] Propagate shrubs and roses by taking softwood cuttings.

FLOWERS

- [ ] Fill gaps in the border, by planting extra annuals and bedding plants.
- [ ] Remove suckers from roses.
- [ ] Cut back oriental poppies.
- [ ] Harvest (and sow) ripe hellebore seed.
- [ ] Plant out canna and lily bulbs that were potted up earlier in the season.
- [ ] Plant borderline hardy ornamentals like agapanthus, salvia and penstemon.
- [ ] Plant out summer bedding.
- [ ] Take insurance cuttings from short-lived perennials like pinks (*right*).

JUNE 2015

TUESDAY

9

WEDNESDAY

10

THURSDAY

11

FRIDAY

12

SATURDAY

13

SUNDAY

14

MONDAY

15

TUESDAY

16

Now is the time to take fuchsia cuttings

your notes

WEATHER:

PLANTS IN BLOOM:

TO DO:

JUNE 2015

WEDNESDAY

17

THURSDAY

18

FRIDAY

19

SATURDAY

20

SUNDAY

21

MONDAY

22

TUESDAY

23

WEDNESDAY

24

AT A GLANCE
JOBS TO DO THIS MONTH

IN THE GREENHOUSE

- [ ] Damp down (*pictured*) and apply shading.
- [ ] Control whitefly.
- [ ] Take cuttings of tender perennials such as fuchsias and pelargoniums.
- [ ] Water and feed plants regularly.
- [ ] Continue to pot up rooted cuttings and pot on young plants and seedlings.

CONTAINERS AND PATIOS

- [ ] Plant up summer containers and hanging baskets, if you haven't already.
- [ ] Keep on top of watering and feeding containers and hanging baskets.
- [ ] Deadhead flowers.
- [ ] Bring out planted hanging baskets that have been sheltering under cover.

WHAT TO PRUNE

- ✓ **Cut spent flower stems of *Euphorbia characias* subsp 'Wulfenii' back to the ground**
- ✓ **Deutzia**
- ✓ **Weigela**
- ✓ **Lilacs**
- ✓ **Trim privet and hedges that are fast-growing**

JUNE 2015

THURSDAY

25

FRIDAY

26

SATURDAY

27

SUNDAY

28

MONDAY

29

TUESDAY

30

Your notes

WEATHER:

PLANTS IN BLOOM:

TO DO:

true or false?

The first ever display of topiary to be exhibited at the Chelsea Flower Show was created by a man called, appropriately, Bert Trimshrub.

(Answer at the bottom of page 105)

Go on, bee friendly!

BEES

The UK's bee population is in trouble – here's how you can give them a hand

THERE HAS been much debate in the media about the alarming decline in the bee population. The one thing we can be sure of is that we're better off with them than without them.

With some thoughtful planning it is possible to provide food all year round for bees that visit our gardens. Planting the right kinds of flowers is the way to achieve this.

Bees prefer flowers with a simple layout of petals, sited in a sunny, sheltered part of the garden. When you're buying from garden centres, many plant labels have a bee friendly sign on them to show that they're suitable.

Many bedding plants, although colourful and sometimes scented, have no pollen or nectar in their flowers so they won't feed bees (*see next page*). If you are still stuck on what plants to choose, walk round your local garden centre and look closely at

which plants in flower are attracting buzzing insects. To check they're suitable, lightly rub your fingertip into the flower, (once the bee has gone)! If pollen is seen on your finger, you're on to a winner.

There are many varieties of bees in the UK, and some will quite happily set up home in the garden, if there is a reliable source of food and somewhere to live. You can buy bee houses from garden centres, but it's easy to make a bee hotel (*see below*) for female Mason bees which lay eggs in hollow stems.

Step by step Build a house for Mason bees

1 Saw a 36 x 4 x ½in (105 x 10 x 1.5cm) plank of untreated wood into 2 x 12in (30cm) lengths and 2 x 8in (20cm) lengths

2 Drill two holes into the edges of each 12in (30cm) piece and attach the 8in (20cm) pieces using wood screws

3 Cut hollow plant stems, such as bamboo (*above*) into 4in (10cm) lengths. To avoid problems, carefully sand off splinters

PLANTS TO GROW

Bees need access to different flowers while they're active outdoors from about March to October. The pollen is collected for the young, whilst the nectar feeds the adult bee.

Spring

- Hellebore (*Helleborus niger, above*)
- Lungwort (*Pulmonaria officinalis*)
- Rosemary (*Rosmarinus officinalis*)
- Pussy willow (*Salix caprea*)
- *Viburnum tinus*
- Early crocus (*Crocus tommasinianus*)
- English bluebell (*Hyacinthoides non-scripta*)
- Crab apple (*Malus sylvestris, below*)

Summer

- Geum *(above)*
- Borage (*Borago officinalis*)
- *Calendula officinalis* (single flowered form)
- Small scabious (*Scabiosa caucasica*)
- Bear's breeches (*Acanthus mollis*)
- The butterfly bush (*Buddleja davidii*)
- Biennial foxglove (*Digitalis purpurea*)
- Masterwort (*Astrantia major, below*)

Encourage bees

1 Stop using insecticides. If you must spray, do it late evening.

2 Choose pollen-rich plants.

3 Plant suitable flowers in a sunny, sheltered spot.

4 If you have the space, set up your own hive, or a bee house.

5 Choose brightly coloured plants; bees are attracted to blue, violet, yellow and white.

6 Plant in clumps. This enables bees to move around them quickly using up less energy.

Bee friendly containers for small spaces

You can also grow suitable bee-friendly plants in containers and hanging baskets. If the pot you are using is big enough, plant a range that will flower throughout the year.

In the container *(below)*, there is thyme, *Allium cowanii*, lavender, cosmos, bronze fennel (at the back of the pot) which will flower late summer, and heather, to flower late winter early spring.

Heathers prefer a slightly acidic soil. As this is a mixed container ericaceous compost was used.

4 Stand the wooden frame on its side, and stack the bamboo lengths inside. When the final ones go in, they will 'lock' together

5 Hang the box by picture fixing hooks onto a sunny fence, sheltered from strong winds, and near a food source

GROW IT

Planting dahlias

FYI

Whether they are in the soil or in a container, dahlia tubers should be planted 4-6in (10-15cm) deep

Fill your garden with the glorious flower shapes of the dahlia

DAHLIAS ARE perennial plants that grow from tubers or seed. There are thousands of varieties available in different sizes, colour and flower shapes. The best time to plant tubers is in late May and early June, after the risk of frost has passed. You can also buy young dahlia plants in pots from garden centres.

You may see dahlias sold as bedding plants. These cultivars have been grown from seed and do not grow very tall.

They will form tubers over the year, and they can be saved for the year after, but for that big hit of colour in your border, choose those grown from tubers in two litre pots from garden centres.

Dahlias grow best in a sunny position in a fertile, moist soil with good drainage. A few days before planting, mix in some well-rotted organic matter to give them a good start. With regular feeding and watering they will produce a spectacular display in any size garden, flowering late into autumn.

To stop dahlia stems breaking they will require staking at planting time; tie in new growth every couple of weeks

Pinching out

Pinch out growing tips on dahlias when they reach a height of about 16in (40cm) to create a bushier plant (*right*). If you want large flowers, pinch out all but three stems.

Stepbystep

1 Dig out a 6in (15cm) hole for tubers. For young plants dig a hole slightly wider and deeper than the pot. Finally, add a sprinkling of general fertiliser.

2 Place the tubers in the hole. If planting containerised dahlias, first water, allow to drain, then plant at the same depth it was in the pot.

3 Place stakes around the tubers (or plant) before you backfill with soil. This ensures the stakes are in position without damaging the tubers or roots.

Using in containers

There are many smaller varieties of dahlia that look great in mixed containers. These can be planted from tubers, or in growth. Choose a container at least 12in (30cm) wide and deep. Plant tubers around 6in (15cm) deep. Set plants at same depth as in pot. Use multipurpose compost and mix in a slow-release feed. Don't let the compost dry out.

Feeding and watering

Dahlias are hungry plants and even after correct planting in fertile soil they will need a liquid feed high in potassium every two weeks, once flower buds appear. Feeding them on a regular basis will encourage more flower buds to come.

Water your dahlias regularly, especially in summer, giving a good soaking of water every couple of days.

Using in borders

Dahlias look stunning in mixed borders. Do allow enough space around them to grow as they can become rather large. Plant in rows 30in (75cm) apart, near the front of borders so they are easily accessible if you want to cut a few flowers for indoors.

One of the best varieties is 'David Howard' – its purple-bronze foliage sets off other plants really well.

Masterclass

June

Home grown Xmas veg

Plan ahead and grow your favourite winter veg for the festive season

T HANKS TO great advancements in seeds and the availability of vegetable plug plants, these days you can grow many types of vegetable for harvesting around Christmas time.

Look for winter-cropping varieties, and those that will grow fast. There are parsnips that if sown now will still be a reasonable size for Christmas, and taste just as sweet. Plug plants can be a good deal if you're just growing a few plants. It's too late for sowing onion seeds or planting sets, but you can grow bulbing spring onions that would be a reasonable substitute.

Here we have chosen a few of the staples, but there are many veggies that you can grow. Kale 'Black Tuscany' is one example – a leafy green that will crop well over the festive period.

If you are leaving parsnips and other edibles in the ground, cover the soil a few days before lifting, with plastic sheeting or cloches, in case the ground freezes.

For Christmas you can produce all the veg for a great lunch. All you will need on the day is a chef to cook it!

FYI
When seedlings are big enough to handle, thin out to the correct spacing to ensure they have room to grow

JUNE

S	M	T	W	T	F	S
	1	2	3	4	5	6
7	8	9	10	11	12	13
14	15	16	17	18	19	20
21	22	23	24	25	26	27
28	29	30				

First (official) day of summer

Start planting!

VEGETABLES TO TRY

1 CARROTS Choose a maincrop variety such as 'Autumn King'. If you are growing them in containers try 'Chantenay'.

To sow, create a fine, level tilth with a rake and water the soil. Place a bamboo cane on its side into the soil to create a thin drill. Sow the seeds along the drill and lightly cover with the soil. Make sure you keep the plot well watered.

2 PARSNIPS Parsnips can be sown now for a crop of baby roots in time for Christmas. On raked, stone-free soil, take out a drill. 'Station'-sow three seeds at 6in (15cm) intervals, cover with a sprinkling of soil and water well. If more than one seed germinates per station, thin down to the strongest seedling.

3 CABBAGES Winter cabbages are a hardy group that will grow well in winter. Look out for 'Tourmaline' from T&M. Sow into a modular tray and thin out when large enough to handle. Pot on into 3in (7cm) pots. Transplant once new growth is seen into their final position, planting deeply to just under their first leaves.

4 HERBS Herbs have many uses at Christmas time. They are best placed in a sheltered spot away from cold winds. Basil will grow indoors from a sowing as late as August. Mint leaves can be frozen before they die down. Herbs like a deep pot filled with well-drained gritty soil.

5 LEEKS Leeks are best grown in open ground or deep raised beds. Now it is best to buy plug plants. To grow them on, make holes 6in (15cm) deep in rows 12in (30cm) apart. Drop the plants into the hole and water in to allow the roots to settle. There is no need to backfill the holes with soil.

6 SWEDE Swede can be sown up to mid June. Sow in shallow drills ½in (1cm) deep. When large enough to handle, thin out seedlings to 6in (15cm) apart. The variety 'Magres' is hardy and mildew-resistant.

Brussels sprouts

Brussels sprouts should be sown in March or April as they are slow-growing, but there are many varieties available as plug plants from garden centres. Plant the plugs in moist, fertile soil, with a spacing of about 2½ft (75cm) between them. Feed in August with Growmore or chicken manure pellets, at the rate of 5oz (150g) per sq m, as they require plenty of nitrogen to grow.

To avoid wind damage to the stems in autumn, support the plants by staking them with canes and mounding soil around the base. Look out for 'Falstaff', a red variety which is decorative enough to grow in borders.

TRUE OR FALSE FROM p99: **FALSE.** But actually his real name – Herbert J. Cutbush – was just as coincidental! He was a nurseryman who appropriately specialised in topiary; he exhibited 'Cutbush's Cut Bushes' around the country, and appeared at the Chelsea Flower Show in 1913.

JULY

Hot days, a shady spot in the garden, a jug of refreshment on the table! July is often one of the hottest months of the year, and is a great time to sit out and enjoy the garden. It is also a very productive month. All the hard work that you put in during the spring now starts to pay off, with so many of the fruit and vegetables ready for harvest. By the end of the month we normally find ourselves swamped with delicious veg such as courgettes, Swiss chard, lettuces, beetroot, French beans and cucumbers.

Wet and humid weather now means that diseases such as potato blight will take hold – and this is the best month for applying sprays to keep the fungus at bay.

July is also an important time to keep on top of weeding, watering and pests. Keep plants looking good by regularly deadheading, and you'll enjoy a longer display of blooms, too. Make sure you keep new plants well watered and hoe off weeds, which thrive in the sunshine.

Roses, fuchsias, clematis, potentillas, hypericums and summer bedding plants are all at their best now.

◁ *Roses are at their best in July: this is the popular shrub rose 'Charles de Mills'*

The garden in *July*

Unusual plants, colours, sculptures and magical features are just some of the features of this, one of the most beautiful gardens in Northern Ireland. Carved from the County Down landscape, the gardens are a mix of formal and informal spaces with many unusual vistas and unique plants from across the world. The trees, plants and shrubs range in ages, size and colour and create a spectacle throughout the year.

HOW TO GET THERE: The garden is situated on Downpatrick Road (A7). Car parking is free. For details of public transport, visit www.nationaltrust.org.uk and follow the links.

OPENING TIMES: Open every day except Christmas Day and Boxing Day. From May to Aug 10am-8pm. From Sept to Oct 10am-6pm. From Nov to Feb 10am-4pm. From Mar to Apr 10am to 6pm.

Rowallane, County Down BT24 7LH

5 top plants for July

1 'Sir John Mills' is a large-flowered hybrid tea-like modern climbing rose.
2 *Cistus* x *purpureus* is a small evergreen shrub with purplish-pink flowers.
3 Deep pink and double, the blooms of the waterlily 'Perry's Pink' are slightly scented.
4 'Stargazer' is one of the most popular of the summer-flowering Oriental hybrid lilies.
5 *Cytisus* 'La Coquette' is a broom with yellow and red flowers – salmon-pink from afar.

This month in
Gardening
history

■ *3 JULY 1806*
The first edible, cultivated strawberry, called 'Keens Seedling', was exhibited by Michael Keens of Isleworth, Surrey.

■ *8 JULY, 1955*
Montagu 'Monty' Denis Wyatt Don – popular presenter of TV's *Gardeners' World* – was born, in Berlin.

■ *12 JULY, 1961*
Green peaches fell on fleeing citizens in a mysterious thundercloud burst over Shreveport, Louisiana, USA. Weathermen blamed a violent updraft causing the peaches to be transported across the countryside... but nobody knows where from.

JULY 2015

WEDNESDAY

1

THURSDAY

2

FRIDAY

3

SATURDAY

4

SUNDAY

5

MONDAY

6

TUESDAY

7

WEDNESDAY

8

AT A GLANCE
JOBS TO DO THIS MONTH

GENERAL TASKS

- [ ] Ask a neighbour to come in and water/deadhead while you're on holiday – group pots together to make it easier; or consider installing a cost-effective automatic watering system.
- [ ] Keep on top of pests and diseases – warm weather tends to make them multiply rapidly.
- [ ] Top up ponds if water levels drop.

TREES, SHRUBS AND CLIMBERS

- [ ] Continue to deadhead repeat-flowering roses; leave once-only roses to develop their colourful autumn hips.
- [ ] Sprinkle fertiliser around roses.
- [ ] Trim conifer hedges, such as privet and *Lonicera nitida*.
- [ ] Water newly planted trees, shrubs and climbers.
- [ ] Take softwood cuttings of shrubs.

Deadhead roses regularly to keep plants tidy – and more blooms coming

JULY 2015

THURSDAY

9

FRIDAY

10

SATURDAY

11

Install a micro-irrigation system to save time

SUNDAY

12

Your notes

WEATHER:

MONDAY

13

PLANTS IN BLOOM:

TUESDAY

14

WEDNESDAY

15

TO DO:

THURSDAY

16

JULY 2015

FRIDAY

17

SATURDAY

18

SUNDAY

19

MONDAY

20

TUESDAY

21

WEDNESDAY

22

THURSDAY

23

FRIDAY

24

AT A GLANCE
JOBS TO DO THIS MONTH

FLOWERS

- [ ] Water and feed herbaceous perennials.
- [ ] Divide irises (*right; see pages 116/117*).
- [ ] Fill gaps in the border with bargain-basement summer bedding.
- [ ] Allow some plants to set seed, for collecting later.
- [ ] Cut back hardy geraniums.
- [ ] Deadhead, water and feed plants in pots and containers regularly.

IN THE GREENHOUSE

- [ ] Pick greenhouse crops regularly.
- [ ] Continue to sow biennial seeds.
- [ ] Keep the greenhouse ventilated; apply more shading paint, if needed.
- [ ] Keep an eye out for pests – red spider mite, mealy bug, aphids and whitefly.

WHAT TO PRUNE

- ✓ **Early summer-flowering shrubs such as weigela and flowering currant**
- ✓ **Clip lavenders once the flowers have finished**
- ✓ **Trim back hedges**
- ✓ **Wisteria – cut back the whippy green shoots of the current year's growth to five or six leaves**

JULY 2015

SATURDAY

25

SUNDAY

26

MONDAY

27

TUESDAY

28

WEDNESDAY

29

THURSDAY

30

FRIDAY

31

Your notes

WEATHER:

PLANTS IN BLOOM:

TO DO:

true or false?

Clematis expert Raymond Evison, one of the best-known faces on the flower show circuit, grows three million clematis plants – every year!

(Answer at the bottom of page 119)

SOW IT

Beautiful biennials

Sow seeds now for a stunning display of colourful flowers next year

DO YOU need a few plants that will flower from spring onwards next year? Biennials, with their showy blooms, fit the bill perfectly.

Biennials are a group of plants that have to overwinter to complete their lifecycle. In the first year they germinate, grow roots and form a clump of leaves. Then, over the colder months, they die back and go dormant. The next year, the plants burst back into life, producing flowers and setting seed before they die.

Many biennials self-seed easily, so the lifecycle starts again. You'll hardly notice, as the new plants grow near to the old parent plant.

You can scatter seeds of biennials, on bare patches of soil between other plants, covering lightly with soil. If you would rather sow in a controlled manner, there are numerous ways to do so. You don't even need to buy special compost, as a multipurpose one is fine to use.

If you haven't grown biennials before, do give them a try as they will give your garden a different dimension – and provide some green foliage over winter.

Biennials look stunning in mixed borders, and many, like the sweet smelling stocks being sown here, are great to use in cut displays

Planting out this autumn

Biennials sown now will quickly germinate, and can easily be planted directly where they are to flower in the garden next year. In colder and exposed regions, and in the north, it is best to get them into their final position by late summer; by early autumn in the south so they can put down roots and establish before the first frost.

5 OF THE BEST BIENNIALS

1

2

3

4

5

1 *Hesperis matronalis* (Sweet rocket)
Sweet rocket will grow in shade or full sun, flowering in May and June. The soil should be well-drained, light and on the dry side.

2 *Matthiola incana* (Stocks)
Heavily scented, they are great to use as a cut flower for indoor displays. Stocks happily grow in moist, fertile soils that are not acidic. Plant and grow them in a sheltered site with full sun.

3 *Verbascum bombyciferum* (Mullein)
With stunning foliage these plants look great used as dot plants. They are drought-tolerant, preferring a light and sandy well-drained soil.

4 *Digitalis purpurea* (Foxglove)
A native flower, the biennial foxglove will grow in almost any soil except very dry or wet locations. You can sow or plant in sun, part or full shade, in exposed or sheltered sites.

5 *Erysimum cheiri* (Wallflower)
Sowing these from seed will give you a wider choice of cultivars than buying bare root plants in autumn from garden centres. Grow in well-drained soil in full sun.

3 Ways to sow

Seed beds

To sow lots of different biennials, create a seedbed in a unused patch of soil. Dig over to remove weeds and large stones. Rake level to create a fine surface, and then sow the seeds in drills, and label. Once germinated and the seedlings are large enough to handle, transplant.

In exposed gardens and those with a slug problem, sow biennials in trays or pots to keep in a coldframe for protection. When large enough, prick out seedlings and pot them up individually. Pot on again so they can produce a large root system, before planting out.

Trays or pots

A different approach

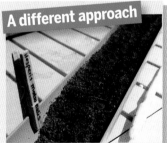

If you are tight on space, sow seeds in guttering, about 3-5ft (1-1.5m) in length. Fill with moist compost and sow in a zigzag pattern. Once seedlings appear, thin out. A few weeks later, make a trench the same size as the guttering and slide plants into the trench.

Dividing irises

WATER IT

FYI
Water newly planted divisions every five days in dry spells, to encourage the rhizomes to establish.

At this time of year you can rejuvenate your tall-bearded irises – and propagate them at the same time!

BEARDED IRISES, with their colourful flowers, are a joy to look at in the spring garden. To keep them flowering well, it is best to divide them every three years, shortly after flowering has finished.

You can tell if they need dividing, because the plants will be generally 'empty' in the middle, with a congestion of surface rhizomes, and surrounded by a ring of leaves.

Not all irises can be divided at this time of year. For example, the clump-forming varieties need to be divided in autumn or spring. For other perennials to divide now, see the list (*opposite page*).

Bearded irises have the reputation of being difficult to grow, especially after division. This is usually as a result of being planted incorrectly.

They grow best in a sunny position, not over-shadowed by other plants. And they should not be planted too deeply – set the rhizomes near to the surface of the soil.

These tidy little iris divisions are being planted at the base of a sunny fence, where they will establish well

Tall bearded iris 'Tintinara'

Stepbystep ➤ Dividing bearded rhizomatous irises

1 Using a garden fork, carefully dig around the plant (avoid damaging the rhizomes). Then gently lift the plant away from the soil.

2 Split each group of leaves with a knife from the main clump. Reduce the leaf size by cutting them back to 6in (15cm) above the rhizome.

3 Trim any long roots seen, then dig a shallow hole for the rhizomes and roots to sit in. Gently replace the soil around them. Firm in, and water.

Other perennials to divide in summer

- ◼ Siberian irises (*Iris sibirica, below*): Clump-forming irises, best divided after flowering
- ◼ Lily-of-the-valley (convallaria): Cut rhizomes into 2-3in (5-8cm) long sections
- ◼ Lungwort (pulmonaria)
- ◼ Barrenwort (epimedium)
- ◼ Blue Himalayan poppy (meconopsis)

What are rhizomes?

Rhizomes are stems that continuously grow underground and can vary in appearance. These stems put out horizontal shoots that break through the soil surface, and they produce adventitious roots at intervals along their lengths. When dividing plants that grow from rhizomes, each section must include roots, young rhizome growth and growth buds.

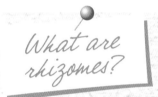

Masterclass

July

Top topiary for cheats!

You can use ivy and hanging baskets to create a cheat's topiary in no time at all!

TOPIARY IS the art of growing dense, leafy plants, trained into 3-dimensional shape or form. Typically, plants such as box and yew are grown into the shapes of birds or animals, or geometrical cubes, globes, pyramids or spirals.

FYI
When 'cheating' with ivy topiary, look out for small leaf varieties such as 'Arran', 'Buttercup', 'Ceridwen' or 'Spetchley'

Creating a good (and recognisable) piece of topiary relies on pruning and training to give shape over a period of time – usually many years.

Almost any woody plant can be 'topiarised'. If a plant can be clipped to a hedge, then it will certainly be good for topiary. Even something like hawthorn can be used, although of course this will be much looser than either box or yew. And it is deciduous, so will lose its leaves each autumn.

Other common topiary evergreens include privet, holly, bay and *Lonicera nitida*.

Two wire hanging baskets, brought together, make a great climbing frame for ivy. Once covered you'll have the perfect topiary ball

Box and yew are definitely the best plants to try, their dense branches bring the best creative scope, easily becoming tails, heads and limbs!

But there is a cheat or two to creating much quicker topiary shapes in the garden that require less input.

Apart from buying a ready-made piece (often very expensive), you can easily create a similar effect with ivy and wire frames. And you won't need to wait years either! Follow our tips here.

JULY

S	M	T	W	T	F	S
			1	2	3	4
5	6	7	8	9	10	11
12	13	14	15	16	17	18
19	20	21	22	23	24	25
26	27	28	29	30	31	

St Swithin's Day

Start tomato harvest!

WIRE FRAME OPTIONS

Simple topiary shapes, such as globes and cubes, can often be trained by eye. However, for more intricate shapes, pre-formed frames can be purchased. They are either made out of galvanised wire, or plastic-coated wire.

Subjects can range from complex animals and people to simpler hearts, pyramids and mushrooms.

The frame is placed over the plant when it is young. As the plant grows it fills the space within the centre of the frame. When shoots start to protrude through the frame, prune or tip them, back to the wire. This maintains the shape.

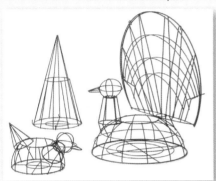

Some of the simpler-shaped frames can be removed (and re-used), but the more complex shapes are intended to be used once, and remain part of the structure. This is not a problem as they tend to remain hidden from view by the foliage.

Buxus topiary

Buxus sempervirens (box) is the traditional subject for creative topiary. Treat yourself to a box cube, ball or pyramid and use this as your 'blank canvas' to get creative with clipping shapes.

It is a forgiving topiary subject, happily re-growing from the hardest of prunes (or misplaced snip of the shears!).

From its regular dimensions and plain sides you will be able to 'sculpt' more interesting shapes.

↑ FRAGILE ☂

Stepbystep ▷ Turning wire hanging baskets into topiary

1 Fix two hanging baskets together with wire, then secure this into the centre of a planted pot containing two or three young ivy plants.

2 Thread the ivy stems up and through the wires of the basket, and continue to do this as they grow. Pinch out tips to encourage side shooting.

3 Regularly weave and tie in wayward stems – in the peak of the growing season growth is fast, so check plants weekly for new shoots to weave into place.

TRUE OR FALSE FROM p113: **TRUE.** Opened in 1984, Raymond's clematis nursery on the Channel Island of Guernsey grows three million plants per year, supplying more than 20 countries around the world.

AUGUST

Traditionally, August is the last month of the British summer. In Scotland it may also be regarded as the first month of autumn!

If the summer has been dry, August is the time of great soil moisture deficits, and if these are also accompanied by bans on the use of hosepipes, garden plants can be put under extreme stress. Certain plants and crops have to be given priority when watering – limited water supplies should not be rationed to all plants, but given to those which will benefit most. Try to use grey water (recycled household water) wherever possible, especially as water butts may be running low.

August is also traditionally holiday-time, so you might need to enlist the help of friends and family to look after the garden while you are away.

Plants giving their all this month include hydrangeas, hardy hibiscus, honeysuckles, yuccas, passionflowers and caryopteris.

◁ *Lettuces are increasingly being grown as decorative plants – both in ornamental and potager gardens, as well as in the traditional veg plot*

The garden in *August*

The landscaped park and gardens of the 18th-century Middleton Hall estate are the setting for this 15-year-old national botanic garden. Near the entrance to the garden is a 'Welsh landscape' with native meadows and woodlands. Then comes the Broadwalk, with a rill which runs down through a geological display of Welsh rocks. The garden's collection of herbaceous plants is planted along its edges, with narrow paths leading into the plantings to facilitate access. There is also a Japanese garden and a herb garden, with an ethnobotanical collection of native pharmacological Welsh plants.

HOW TO GET THERE: The garden is seven miles east of Carmarthen, off the A48. For details of public transport, visit www.gardenofwales.org.uk and follow the links.

OPENING TIMES: Open every day except Christmas Eve and Christmas Day. 10am–6pm (4.30pm during British Winter Time).

The National Botanic Garden of Wales, Carmarthen SA32 8HN

5 top plants for August

1 'Livingstone daisy' (or *Mesembryanthemum criniflorum*) is a tender summer succulent.
2 Another succulent, this is the sun rose, or portulaca.
3 *Fuchsia* 'Heidi Ann' is a tender fuchsia for summer bedding or pots.
4 Coleus (solenostemon) produce some of the brightest and most colourful of summer foliage.
5 There are many bedding geraniums – this is *Pelargonium* 'Flower Fairy White Splash'.

This month in
Gardening
history

■ *4 AUGUST, 1996*
Geoff Hamilton (*below*), writer, presenter of BBC 2's *Gardener's World* and arguably the nation's most famous gardener at the time, died whilst on a charity bike ride in Wales.

■ *17 AUGUST, 1671*
The garden at Vaux-le-Vicomte, 55 miles southeast of Paris, had its grand opening. It was the first major garden design by Andre le Notre, the favourite landscape architect of the French Royal household.

■ *29 AUGUST, 1673*
The Apothecaries' Company first signed the lease on the Chelsea Physic Garden at Cheyne Walk in London.

123

AUGUST 2015

SATURDAY

1

SUNDAY

2

MONDAY

3

TUESDAY

4

WEDNESDAY

5

THURSDAY

6

FRIDAY

7

SATURDAY

8

AT A GLANCE
JOBS TO DO THIS MONTH

GENERAL TASKS

☐ Watch out for powdery mildew on honeysuckle and roses.

☐ Keep an eye out for slugs in cool, wet weather; apply slug controls.

☐ Keep plants well watered and fed, particularly those in containers.

☐ Deadhead flowers to stop seed setting and encourage more blooms.

☐ Control vine weevil in containers.

☐ Mow lawns, but don't feed or water.

☐ Clear out yellow or decomposing water lily leaves from ponds.

☐ Top up ponds (ideally with rainwater), especially if you're going on holiday.

TREES, SHRUBS AND CLIMBERS

☐ Trim hedges, such as hornbeam, Leyland cypress, beech and thuja.

☐ Feed camellias and rhododendrons and water well.

☐ Take semi-ripe cuttings of herbs.

☐ Propagate clematis by layering.

Control vine veevil in containers

AUGUST 2015

SUNDAY

9

MONDAY

10

TUESDAY

11

WEDNESDAY

12

THURSDAY

13

FRIDAY

14

SATURDAY

15

SUNDAY

16

After a period of hot weather, top up ponds

Your notes

WEATHER:

PLANTS IN BLOOM:

TO DO:

AUGUST 2015

MONDAY

17

TUESDAY

18

WEDNESDAY

19

THURSDAY

20

FRIDAY

21

SATURDAY

22

SUNDAY

23

MONDAY

24

AT A GLANCE
JOBS TO DO THIS MONTH

 **FLOWERS**

- Set earwig traps around dahlias (*right*) and chrysanths.
- Trim back perennials that have flopped over.
- Save seed from hardy bulbs, annuals, bulbs and perennials.
- Pot up self-sown seedlings.
- Plant autumn-flowering bulbs.
- Take cuttings of alpines.

IN THE GREENHOUSE

- Ventilate the greenhouse daily.
- The traditional month for taking cuttings of pelargoniums and fuchsias.
- You can start potting up hyacinths for Christmas flowers.

CONTAINERS AND PATIOS

- Keep watering and feeding containers and hanging baskets.

WHAT TO PRUNE

✓ **Rambling roses**

✓ **Trim lavender, rosemary and santolina**

✓ **Finish summer pruning of wisteria**

AUGUST 2015

TUESDAY

25

WEDNESDAY

26

THURSDAY

27

FRIDAY

28

SATURDAY

29

SUNDAY

30

MONDAY

31

Your notes

WEATHER:

PLANTS IN BLOOM:

TO DO:

true or false?

The total area of land given over to gardens in the UK is equal to an area the size of the Isle of Wight (*pictured*).

(Answer at the bottom of page 133)

GROW IT

Tropical containers

FYI
Group tropical plants together in the garden centre, so you can see which ones work well together

Create a jungle look in pots for a colourful August Bank Holiday display

TROPICAL PLANTS are native to regions surrounding the Equator, and have growing requirements specific to their location. Many of them need warm, humid conditions, but they will grow in the UK with the correct care.

Setting tropical plants in attractive containers allows you to display them outdoors in the summer. You can then carry on growing them indoors as the weather gets colder – most of them are not hardy below 10°C (50°F).

When choosing plants for a mixed container display, be sure they all have the same watering and compost requirements. This will ensure that the whole display thrives.

If your budget can only stretch to a couple of tropical plants, group them with hot looking colourful native and Mediterranean plants to maintain the look. Pelargonium, miniature roses and agapanthus all work well.

So grab an empty container and get scouting the garden centre – you'll soon be enjoying a taste of the tropics in your own back garden. Here's how to do it.

To keep these tropical plants growing all year, move them to a frost-free site or indoors when the weather turns colder

✔ Tips on planting

Tropical plants in containers will need adequate drainage so their roots do not rot. Add cut up plastic pot holders or used polystyrene bedding trays to the bottom of the pot before planting to aid water drainage.

Use a loam-based compost such as John Innes No2, or No3 for mature specimens. Mix in some horticultural grit if the compost feels too heavy. Some plants prefer ericaceous compost; check labels for their exact requirements.

Watering will depend on the variety of plant, as many have very different needs. Always check the label for the amount of watering required. Mist large leaves daily and place pots on watering trays filled with gravel and water, to increase humidity.

Plunge planting

Plunge planting is the practice of burying a potted plant in compost or soil, up to its rim. This system works well with tropical plants you need to bring indoors at a later date. Use a decorative stone or terracotta container for the outside pot, and you can easily change the planting in the autumn.

6 TROPICAL PLANTS FOR POTS

1 Canna
Plant using a John Innes No. 3 compost. To encourage more flowers on this tender perennial, deadhead promptly once blooms have finished. Prune back old flower spikes to a side shoot, to encourage new ones.

2 Bananas (Musa)
With wonderful different coloured foliage, banana plants look stunning in containers. Use a John Innes No.3 mixed with horticultural grit. Water and feed weekly with a liquid fertiliser, and mist leaves daily.

3 Coconut palm
These plants require consistently warm temperatures; bring indoors when the temperature is in single figures. Plant in well-drained even slightly sandy compost. Mist and water leaves daily.

4 Strelitzia
Commonly know as the bird of paradise, these plants will flower after their third year. Allow the compost to almost dry out before watering, and feed weekly with a general liquid fertiliser until autumn.

5 Spathiphyllum
The peace lily prefers a site that is in part shade. Plant in a container using either loam based or loam-free (multipurpose) compost. Mist the leaves daily and apply a balanced liquid feed monthly.

6 Coleus
Coleus plants come in a wide range of different colours. Plant in a free-draining multipurpose compost, sited in sun or part shade. Pinch out shoot tips to promote side growths to make a bushy plant.

GROW IT

Take cuttings of hardy azaleas

Increase your stock of evergreen azleas by taking cuttings now

A ZALEAS ARE colourful flowering shrubs that bloom in spring and early summer. Part of the rhododendron family, they can be deciduous or evergreen, growing best in partial shade in well-drained, acidic soil.

Semi-ripe cuttings, (sometimes referred to as 'semi-mature' cuttings) can be taken from the evergreen varieties now. The stems are beginning to become woody, but are still able to bend slightly. This material is less likely to wilt than softwood cuttings, but may take longer to root. To overcome this problem it is best to wound the cuttings before planting (*see opposite*). Doing so will speed up the development of roots and increase the uptake of water by the new plants.

Azalea cuttings may take up to eight weeks to root. Once rooted, pot up individually and over winter in a cold frame to plant out next spring.

FYI

Once cuttings are inserted into the compost, place them out of direct light so they do not lose moisture

Azaleas are compact plants and grow well in containers filled with ericaceous compost. Take cuttings from the new season's growth

Keeping cuttings material fresh

If the cuttings cannot be planted straight away, place them in a plastic bag and spray the material with water. Place the bag in a fridge until you are ready, but for no longer than a day.

Step by step ▸ How to take azalea cuttings

1 Mix together one part perlite to three parts ericaceous compost and fill small pots – about 3in (7.5cm)pots – with the planting medium. Water the mixture and allow to drain.

2 Select a healthy flexible, but maturing stem, about 2-5in (5-12cm) long and cut just above a leaf or node. Then trim the cutting to just below the bottom leaf or node.

3 Remove all the leaves, except for the cluster of terminal leaves at the top. Then carefully cut away a 1in (2.5cm) sliver of bark with a sharp, clean knife to reveal the pithy flesh.

4 Dip the ends in rooting compound and insert them around the edges of the pots. Water well, then put the pots in a heated propagator or cover with a cloche or polythene bag.

'Charlotte Morgan' is one of the lovely azaleas hybrids bred by noted New Forest breeder George Hyde

Masterclass

August

Watering made easy

The right hose and attachments will make light work of watering in summer

WATERING THE garden is one of those mundane but vital tasks. It's not much fun, but has to be done. Many gardeners, by necessity, do it in a mad rush before going to work in the morning, often leaving the hose strewn across the garden!

If you don't get around to watering (or putting the hose away!) it's down to lack of time, but for some people, physical constraints are often a barrier to effective watering.

If you are less able, look at your garden with a view to making things easier – shrub borders instead of bedding displays for example.

Often, running a hose around the garden isn't a problem, but reeling back 60ft (18m) of hose at ground level can be hard and heavy work, and so can be difficult. A wall-hung system may be the answer, but be careful – these may still require a manual rewind.

Several brands - Gardena,

A self-retracting hose reel system is ideal for many

Kingfisher, Hozelock – offer easy auto reels.

Here we're installing a Hozelock Auto Reel. The hose is pulled from the reel and clicks into place. When it's time to put it away, a simple tug unlatches the drum, and an automatic rewind system takes over to neatly pull the hose back onto the reel, without kinks, tangles or knots.

If reeling in the hose after watering is a struggle for you, try an auto reel system yourself. Installation is easy....

Make watering even easier

The right attachment also makes watering easier. Hozelock's Flexi Spray won the RHS Chelsea Flower Show Product of the Year award. It can even be moulded for a range of hands-free functions.

Wrap it around a tool handle for targeted watering (*below*); straighten the lance and bend the head and you have the perfect hanging basket waterer. It can even be set up as a sprinkler to keep lawns green in summer heat.

AUGUST

S	M	T	W	T	F	S
						1
2	3	4	5	6	7	8
9	10	11	12	13	14	15
16	17	18	19	20	21	22
23	24	25	26	27	28	29
30	31					

Bank Holiday

Stepbystep Wall mounting a hose reel

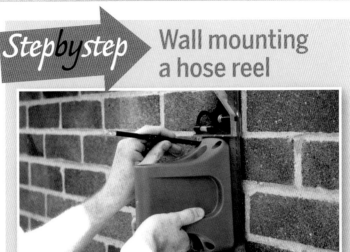

1 The wall-mounted bracket can be fixed at a height to suit your needs. Use a spirit level and mark the screw holes on the wall. Drill the holes, insert rawlplugs and screw to the wall.

2 The lightweight drum is easily fixed to the bracket. Offer up the drum and insert the pin through both. Ahead of winter it can be easily removed and stored to prevent weathering .

3 With the drum in place, a front panel is removed to connect the reel to the outlet hose running from the garden tap. Pop the panel back on and you're set for some easy watering.

TRUE OR FALSE FROM p127: **FALSE.** The total area of gardens throughout the UK equals 4,300km², which is more than 10 times the size of the Isle of Wight (which is 'just' 380km²). The total garden area is actually bigger than the county of Somerset.

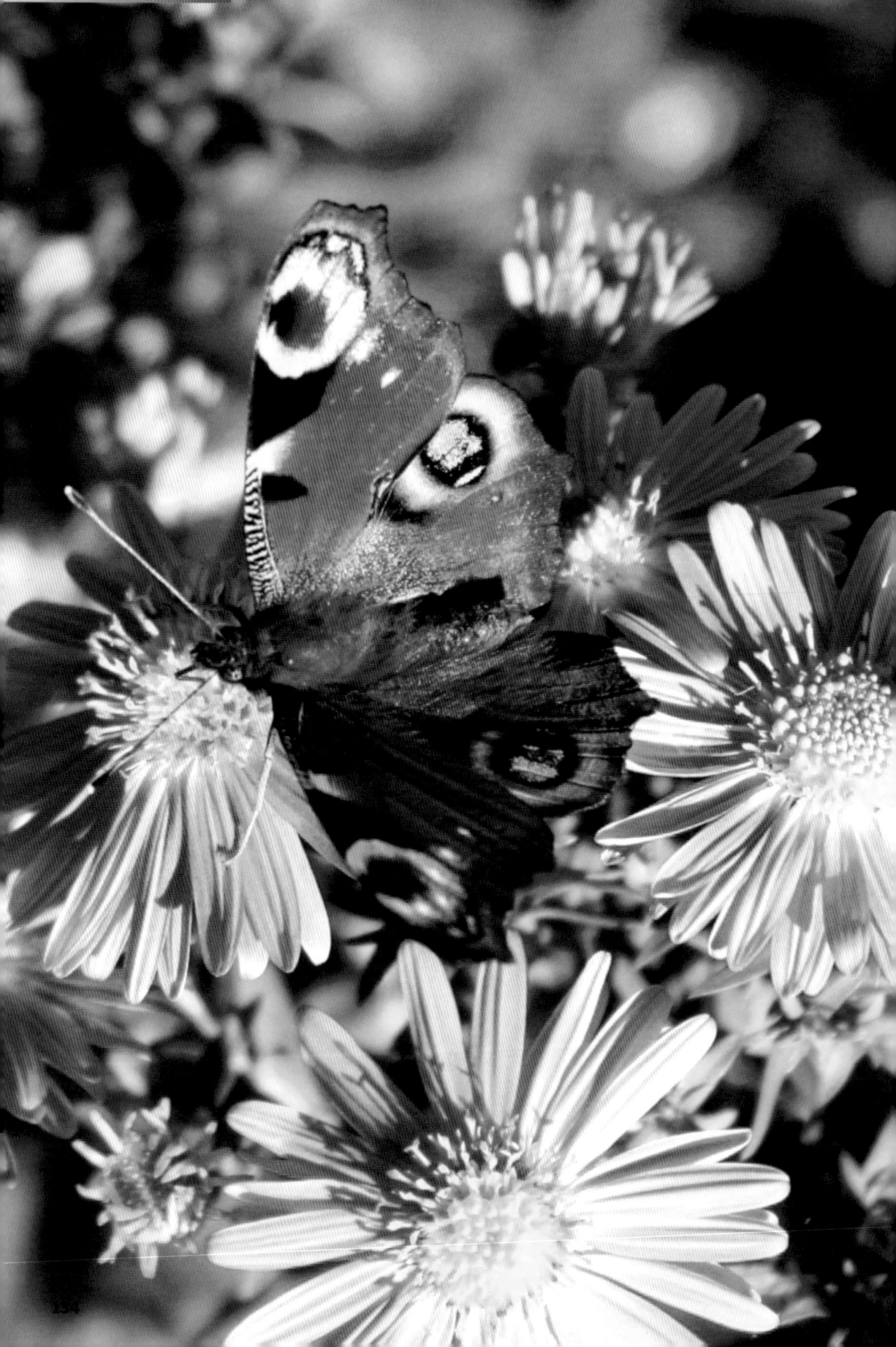

SEPTEMBER

The days are generally cooler now, and are noticeably shorter. Although inland gales are more likely to occur later in the year, winds in September are generally stronger than those prevailing in the summer.

Good, carefully planned shelter from the wind is essential for successful gardening, especially in coastal regions, on hills, or on extensive flat areas where there is little natural obstruction to the flow of the wind.

While there's not as much to do in the ornamental garden at this time of the year, if you have a fruit or vegetable patch, you'll be harvesting lots of produce. It's also time to get out and start planting spring-flowering bulbs for next year.

All of the plants flowering in August are likely to be looking decent now as well, but there will certainly be an 'end-of-the-growing-year' feel to the garden – so you should make the most of any remaining warmth while you can!

◁ *Michaelmas daisies (forms of aster) are at their best in late summer and early autumn – and they provide a haven for butterflies*

The garden in *September*

GARDEN TO VISIT

Mount Stewart is one of the most unusual gardens in the National Trust's ownership. The mild climate of Strangford Lough allows high levels of planting experimentation. The formal areas exude a strong Mediterranean feel and resemble an Italian villa landscape; and the wooded areas support a range of plants from all corners of the world, ensuring something to see, whatever the season.

HOW TO GET THERE: The garden is situated on the Newtownards to Portaferry road, the A20, 15 miles south-east of Belfast. Car parking is free. For details of public transport, visit www.nationaltrust.org.uk and follow the links.

OPENING TIMES: Open every day except Christmas Day and Boxing Day. 8 Mar to 2 Nov 10am – 5pm; 3 Nov to 7 Mar 10am – 4pm.

Mount Stewart, County Down BT22 2AD

5 top plants for September

1 *Crocosmia* 'Lucifer' is an attractive perennial for late summer, with deep red flowers.
2 *Phormium* 'Cream Delight' has spiky, variegated leaves.
3 *Eriophorum angustifolium* is a moisture-lover, also known as cotton grass.
4 *Diascia rigescens* is a spreading semi-evergreen perennial with two-spurred flowers in shades of pink.
5 *Sedum* 'Autumn Joy' is a late-summer plant for attracting butterflies and bees; best at the front of a border.

This month in
Gardening
history

■ *13 SEPT, 1879*
Punch magazine published a cartoon about the disturbance caused by the gardener with his noisy lawnmower, proving that the machine had become such an essential piece of equipment for upper and middle-class homes.

■ *17 SEPT, 1671*
The garden at Vaux-le-Vicomte, 55 miles southeast of Paris, had its grand opening. It was the first major garden design by Andre le Notre, the favourite landscape architect of the French Royal household.

■ *25 SEPT, 1878*
The International Potato Exhibition was held at Crystal Palace.

SEPTEMBER 2015

TUESDAY

1

WEDNESDAY

2

THURSDAY

3

FRIDAY

4

SATURDAY

5

SUNDAY

6

MONDAY

7

TUESDAY

8

AT A GLANCE
JOBS TO DO THIS MONTH

GENERAL TASKS

- [ ] Buy or make a compost bin for all the autumn debris.
- [ ] Cover ponds with netting to prevent falling leaves entering the water.

LAWNS

- [ ] Rake out moss where it is growing heavily (*right*).
- [ ] Aerate and top-dress.
- [ ] Feed lawns with autumn fertiliser.

TREES, SHRUBS AND CLIMBERS

- [ ] Plant pot-grown trees and shrubs.
- [ ] Plant and move evergreens.
- [ ] Trim hedges like hornbeam, Leyland cypress, beech, thuja, *Lonicera nitida* and privet.

Give hornbeam hedges a final trim

SEPTEMBER 2015

WEDNESDAY

9

THURSDAY

10

FRIDAY

11

SATURDAY

12

SUNDAY

13

MONDAY

14

TUESDAY

15

WEDNESDAY

16

Your notes

WEATHER:

PLANTS IN BLOOM:

TO DO:

Clear away spent summer flowers

SEPTEMBER 2015

THURSDAY

17

FRIDAY

18

SATURDAY

19

SUNDAY

20

MONDAY

21

TUESDAY

22

WEDNESDAY

23

THURSDAY

24

AT A GLANCE
JOBS TO DO THIS MONTH

 **FLOWERS**

☐ Plant new perennials.

☐ Cut down and divide existing perennials.

☐ Plant daffodils and other spring bulbs.

☐ Sow hardy annuals outside for early flowering next year (*above*).

☐ Plant out spring-flowering biennials and winter-flowering pansies.

☐ Clear out summer bedding as it comes to an end.

☐ Continue to collect seed from perennials and alpines.

IN THE GREENHOUSE

☐ Move pots of tender plants like fuchsias and pelargoniums undercover.

☐ Sow hardy annuals in pots.

☐ Plant early spring bulbs in pots.

☐ Reduce watering and feeding of all greenhouse and container plants.

WHAT TO PRUNE

✓ **Start pruning climbing roses**

✓ **Prune lavender to maintain its shape**

✓ **Remove suckers from shrubs and the base of trees**

✓ **Prune tall roses to reduce windrock**

SEPTEMBER 2015

FRIDAY

25

SATURDAY

26

SUNDAY

27

MONDAY

28

TUESDAY

29

WEDNESDAY

30

Your notes

WEATHER:

PLANTS IN BLOOM:

TO DO:

true or false?

TV gardener Rachel de Thame (*pictured*) is also an expert cook and author of a cookery book *Less Meat, More Veg*.

(Answer at the bottom of page 147)

Bulb planting for colour

WATER IT

Plant bulbs for glorious spring and summer colour in the garden next year

GARDEN CENTRES are now bulging at the seams with different varieties of bulbs, which will flower from very early next spring through to late summer. Buying them sooner rather than later will ensure you get the best quality bulbs, as well as your choice of varieties.

Now is the perfect time to plant most bulbs, as the soil is moist and warm. Tulips are different in that they can be planted later in the autumn, practically up until Christmas time.

Bulbs will grow in most soil types, as long as it is not waterlogged, which can cause the bulbs to rot or produce small, weak flowers. To improve drainage on heavy soils, dig in some horticultural grit prior to planting.

It's not just spring flowering bulbs that can be planted in autumn; hardy summer-flowering bulbs can be planted as well. Planting these now will give them as much time as possible to produce beautiful, large flowers next year (see list below).

It always pays to be pennywise in the garden. Buy cheap, large bags of bulbs for mass bedding, or team up with neighbours to share the price – and planting – workload!

FYI
If you can't tell which way up a bulb should be planted, place it on its side: the stem and roots will grow in the right directions

When choosing bulbs look for the largest one you can find in that variety. Small bulbs may not flower the first year after planting, or they may produce small, weak blooms. Gently feel the bulbs and discard any that are soft or show signs of rotting and mould.

Summer flowering

Hardy summer bulbs that can be planted in September and October include:

- **Alliums:** *(pictured)* **Flower better in part shade**
- Crocosmia: Grow in sun or part shade
- **Lilies: Plant in shaded soil, but where flowers will be in the sun**
- Bearded Iris: Grow in full sun
- **Sicilian honey garlic (nectaroscordum): Full sun to part shade**

'X' marks the spot

To prevent damage or disturbance when winter digging and planting, mark the centre of the area planted with bulbs with a label, so you know where they are. Be careful not to spike them. If you want something a little more showy than a plant label, decorative bulb markers are available from garden centres.

Spring flowering bulbs

Spring flowering bulbs to plant now include:

- Crocus: (*right*) Grow in full sun or part shade in groups, to look natural
- Daffodil: Plant in sun or light shade
- Snake's head fritillary: Grows best in full sun or part shade
- Snowdrops: Plant in part or dappled shade
- Outdoor hyacinth: Best in full sun, but will tolerate a little shade
- Lily-of-the-valley: Best in part or full shade
- Winter aconite: Plant in sun or part shade
- Bluebell: Best grown in dappled or part shade
- Russian snowdrop (puschkinia): Grow in full sun or part shade

Planting depths

Pictured right is a guide to bulb planting depths, but don't worry if you cannot get it exactly right; many of us don't have the time to measure exact spacing and depths. As a general rule, however, bulbs should be planted in a hole three or four times as deep as the bulb itself. The space between should be about twice the width.

Bulb planting can be back-breaking work. If you find digging difficult, bulb planters, especially those with long handles, may make the task of planting easier.

Stop squirrel damage

Bulbs are generally hardy and disease-resistant, but newly planted ones are at risk of being damaged by squirrels. Tulips and crocuses are high on the squirrel's list for a tasty treat. To reduce the risk of bulbs being unearthed, once planted lay a piece of chicken wire over the top, covering with a thin layer of soil or compost.

Pots and pots of runner beans!

Amateur Gardening editor **Tim Rumball** shares his experience of growing runner bean crops in containers

ANY VEG or fruit can be grown in a pot... but some will grow better than others. I've never had big crops from runner beans in containers, but I gave up my allotment, so pots it has to be.

Climbing runner beans are easy to grow in soil in the open garden, but in a container it's not so simple. Even putting up a wigwam of canes is tricky – they waggle around alarmingly. But note that any canes less than 8ft (2.4m) long will be too short.

I'm not a fan of dwarf runner beans such as 'Hestia', sold for pot growing. In my experience they don't crop for long and the beans can be coarse – to my taste.

Most recently I've grown 'Tenderstar' with bicoloured red and white flowers, and white flowered 'Moonlight'– both self-fertile recent introductions from Thompson & Morgan. Seeds were sown 1in (2.5cm) deep in small pots filled with moist multipurpose compost in mid-April. Popped in a heated propagator in the frost-free greenhouse (a warm, bright windowsill would do) they germinated quickly and were ready for planting out in my big pot – 2 plants per cane – in mid-May after acclimatisation to outdoor conditions (hardening-off).

I live on the south coast. However, if you live in a colder spot, wait until early June to set the plants out.

Anyway, I filled a big 30 x 30in (68 x 68cm) pot with used potting compost mixed with some fresh multipurpose, as well as two buckets of well rotted manure and two handfuls of blood, fish and bone fertiliser. A wigwam of six canes was pushed in deep then tied tightly at the top with rotproof garden twine. The plants were set in the pot, one variety either side, positioned in a sheltered, sunny spot.

Then it's water, water, water – the compost dries out fast. Check every day, and give a liquid tomato feed once a week when flowering starts.

Both varieties cropped steadily. Beans were short – 6-10in (15-25cm) – and early pickings were a bit tough, but they tasted fine. Cropping went on for about seven weeks, on and off from mid July. I picked beans daily, storing them in the fridge for up to five days.

FYI
Tie the bean growths to the canes initially, after which they can be left to climb up them naturally

Beans in pots step-by-step

- **Sow seeds, one per small pot filled with multipurpose compost, in late April**
- Set pots on a warm, bright windowsill
- **Harden off plants in late May before planting out**
- Fill a large pot (20litres or more) with compost and well rotted manure, adding blood, fish and bone fertiliser, or similar
- **Set a wigwam of 8ft (2.4m) canes in the pot, tied at the top with rot-proof twine**
- Set two plants at the base of each cane and water in well
- **Water daily in season, feed once a week with high potash fertiliser (tomato feed) as flowers appear**
- Pick beans while they are young and tender

Supports

Twelve plants set at the feet of six 8ft (2.4m) canes in a large pot gave fair pickings over about seven weeks

Harvest time!

Pick beans when the pods are 6-8in (15-20cm) long ⟶

Masterclass

September

Sowing hardy annuals

Sow hardy annuals now for an early flower display next year

FYI
When thinning out seedlings pot any extras up for transplanting out in spring to fill any bare patches

A NNUALS ARE plants that flower, set seed and die in one year. In early autumn it is possible to sow the hardy varieties for an early flowering display next year.

Sowing them at this time of year, while the soil is warm and moist, enables the seeds to germinate quickly, developing a strong root system. Hardy annuals can survive frosts, but as we all know our winter and spring climate can be very erratic so it is still worth protecting them during severe weather (*see panel right*).

Although many of these plants are native to the UK and can tolerate poor soils, for a better flowering display, prep the sowing site a week before, by adding organic matter such as compost, with a sprinkling of Growmore fertiliser. Most prefer to grow in a sheltered, sunny spot, especially the taller

If you don't have the space to sow hardy annuals in drifts, sow a few between late flowering perennials for early colour next year

varieties, whose stems can be damaged by strong winds.

Sow hardy annuals outdoors by direct sowing in drills, or by broadcast sowing. Broadcast sowing is simply scattering the seeds over a patch of bare soil. Whichever way you choose to sow, you'll be rewarded with a colourful early summer display.

SEPTEMBER

S	M	T	W	T	F	S
		1	2	3	4	5
6	7	8	9	10	11	12
13	14	15	16	17	18	19
20	21	22	23	24	25	26
27	28	29	30			

Sharpen winter tools

Start autumn planting!

Step by step
Sowing hardy annuals in drifts by variety

1 Prepare the soil by removing weeds and large stones. Stand on a board to avoid compaction of the soil and rake level to create a fine tilth.

2 Mark out areas with sand where each variety is to be sown. Press a bamboo cane into the soil to create shallow drills about 3in (7.5cm) apart.

3 Sow the seeds in the drills. Sow the tallest varieties at the back. Cover with a sprinkling of soil, label each section and then water in.

Protecting seeds

Birds and some small mammals may attack the seeds before they have the chance to germinate. Protect them after sowing by placing either chicken wire or twiggy branches over the top of them.

Autumn frosts and prolonged rain may also damage the seedlings, once germinated, cover with a layer of horticultural fleece if severe weather is forecast over winter and early spring.

Annuals with bulbs

Sow hardy annuals over spring- and summer-flowering bulbs to create a continuous display of colour next year

1 First, plant the bulbs of your choice at the correct depth and spacing in well-drained fertile soil. We are planting alliums and sowing the hardy cornflower, both of which will bloom around about the same time.

2 Gently cover the bulbs with soil and water in, using a fine rose watering can, and leave to drain. Gently rake over the soil to remove stones and weeds, creating a fine tilth without disturbing the bulbs.

3 Broadcast-sow the seeds of your choice over the raked soil. Gently cover the seeds by brushing over with soil using your hand. Label the area, ensuring the bulb and flowers are both documented.

TRUE OR FALSE FROM p141: **FALSE.** The cookery expert who has brought out a book of this name is Rachel de Thample – *not* Rachel de Thame. Close, but not quite there!

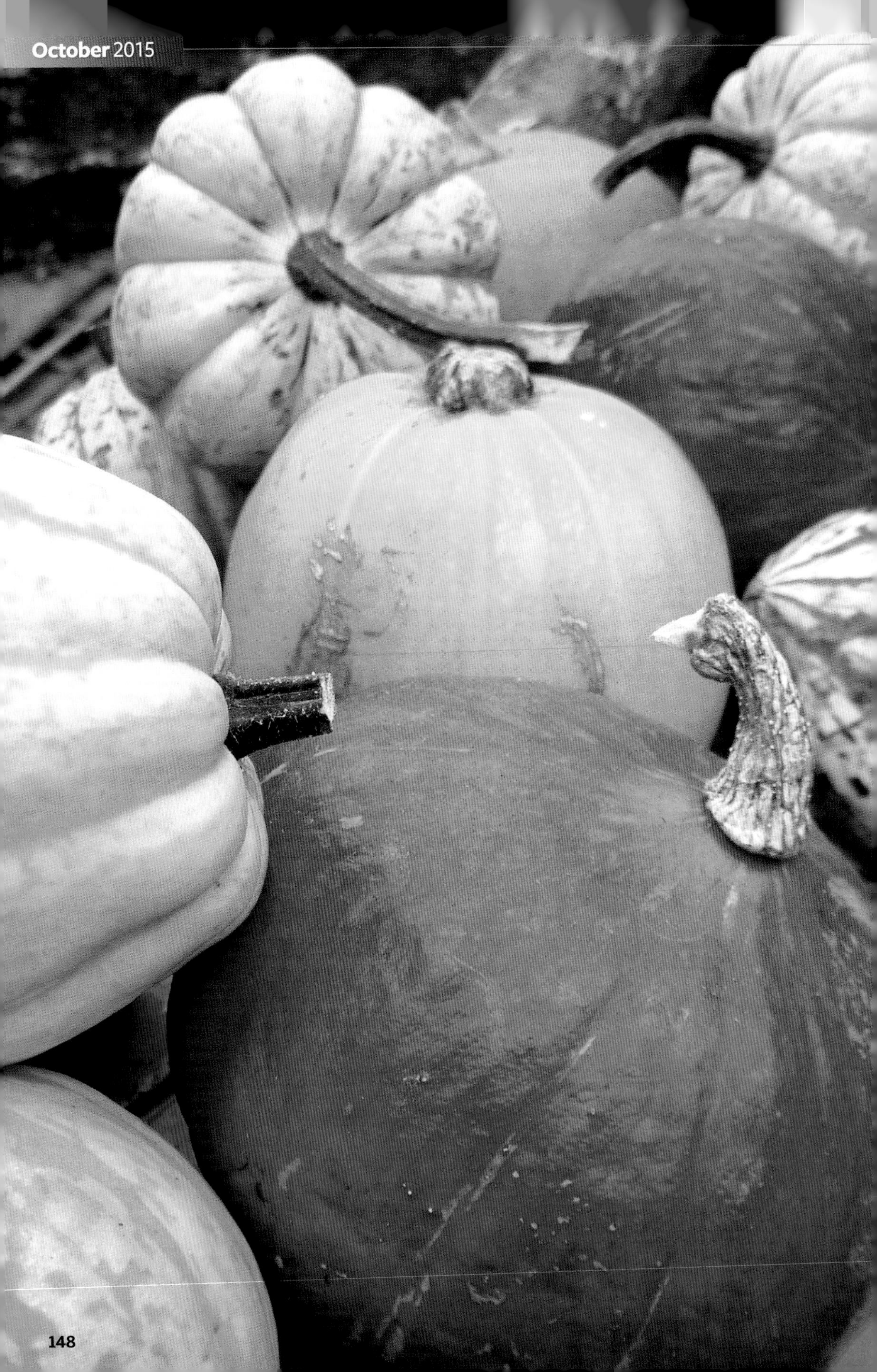

OCTOBER

In autumn, not only are the days closing in, but the conditions suitable for outdoor work are getting less frequent. This means that the first favourable opportunities must be taken.

It is, however, a beautiful time of year, with the trees changing colour. Sometimes it may seem pointless, raking up fallen leaves in the garden, when we know full well that the wind will blow even more down, but just think of all the lovely leafmould you can make!

Autumn digging is important, not only because it cleans the ground of annual weeds, and buries crop residues, but also because it enables the winter frosts to penetrate the rough soil surface, and so break up the larger clods of soil in a very efficient manner, to provide a workable tilth.

Plants of note in October include those with autumn leaf tints and decorative fruits, such as acers, berberis, cotoneaster, prunus and deciduous azaleas.

◁ *With generally warmer summers, and better plant breeding, pumpkins are now a familiar sight in British gardens – and they are synonymous with Halloween, at the end of October*

The garden in
October

GARDEN
TO
VISIT

Harlow Carr is a garden dominated by water, stone and woodland and is very much part of the surrounding Yorkshire landscape. Wander through the tranquil surroundings of this 58 acre (23ha) garden and gain ideas for your own borders. Along the dramatic Main Borders there is contemporary planting to suit the challenging growing conditions. You can pick up the latest tips and growing techniques in the recently expanded Kitchen Garden featuring raised beds, fruit trees and a forager's garden. Don't miss the magnificent Alpine House, too.

HOW TO GET THERE: The garden is situated on Crag Lane, off Otley Road (B6162) about a mile and a half from the centre of Harrogate. Car parking is free. For details of public transport, visit www.rhs.org.uk/ Gardens and follow the links.

OPENING TIMES: Open every day except Christmas Day. 1 Mar to 8 Nov 9.30am-6pm; 9 Nov to 28 Feb 9.30am-4pm. Last admission one hour before closing.

RHS Garden Harlow Carr, North Yorkshire HG3 1UE

5 top plants for October

1 The Guelder rose (*Viburnum opulus*) produces bright red autumn berries.
2 *Chrysanthmum* Single Spray 'Daniele Purple' is great for a patio container.
3 *Gentiana* 'Marsha' is one of the larger-flowered forms, giving a bright splash of blue in autumn.
4 Often known as 'naked ladies' or 'autumn crocus', *Colchicum speciosum* 'Atrorubens' is a stunning bulb.
5 *Schizostylis* 'Viscountess Byng' has bright pink autumn flowers.

This month in
Gardening
history

■ *10 OCTOBER 1908*
The National Chrysanthemum Society finally succumbed to pressure to consider moving their shows to the RHS Hall at Westminster.

■ *16 OCTOBER, 1987*
A Great Storm raged in Southern England. One of the most famous UK television quotes came from weatherman Michael Fish when he said: "A lady phoned in to the BBC to say that there was a hurricane on the way. Well, there isn't..."

■ *20 OCTOBER, 1962*
At a garden trade meeting, a Mr Bygrave reported on the American innovation of nurseries growing plants in containers in order to sell to the public. Before this, plants had been dug up from the soil. This new way revolutionised gardening.

OCTOBER 2015

THURSDAY

1

FRIDAY

2

SATURDAY

3

SUNDAY

4

MONDAY

5

TUESDAY

6

WEDNESDAY

7

THURSDAY

8

AT A GLANCE
JOBS TO DO THIS MONTH

GENERAL TASKS

☐ Tidy borders and use the debris to make garden compost.

☐ Remove fallen leaves from lawns, the crowns of plants and pathways. Use them to make leaf mould.

☐ Reduce fish feeding (*below*) and cut aquatic plants that have gone over.

☐ Clean out the sludge at the bottom of ponds (once every five or six years).

LAWNS

☐ Reduce mowing frequency and raise the blades.

☐ Carry out autumn lawn care if you didn't get around to it last month.

TREES, SHRUBS AND CLIMBERS

☐ Prepare ground for planting bare-root trees and shrubs next month.

Sweep toadstools and fairy rings off the lawn

OCTOBER 2015

FRIDAY

9

SATURDAY

10

SUNDAY

11

MONDAY

12

TUESDAY

13

WEDNESDAY

14

THURSDAY

15

FRIDAY

16

Weed and spruce up paths and driveways

your notes

WEATHER:

PLANTS IN BLOOM:

TO DO:

OCTOBER 2015

SATURDAY
17

SUNDAY
18

MONDAY
19

TUESDAY
20

WEDNESDAY
21

THURSDAY
22

FRIDAY
23

SATURDAY
24

AT A GLANCE
JOBS TO DO THIS MONTH

 **FLOWERS**

- [ ] Dry attractive seedheads.
- [ ] Cut back herbaceous perennials that have finished flowering; plant new ones.
- [ ] Divide perennials (leave later-flowering ones like asters until the spring).
- [ ] If in a cold region, lift and store gladioli, dahlias, eucomis and tigridia.
- [ ] Move tender plants undercover.
- [ ] Plant new peonies and divide old ones.

IN THE GREENHOUSE

- [ ] Pot up cuttings taken in the summer.
- [ ] Pot up herbs like parsley and mint for winter use (*right*).
- [ ] If forced bulbs have top growth and root growth, bring them into the light.

CONTAINERS AND PATIOS

- [ ] Plant up a winter container of pansies and polyanthus for colour on the patio.

WHAT TO PRUNE

✓ **Cut buddleja and lavatera back by half (hard prune in the spring)**

✓ **Continue pruning climbing roses**

✓ **Last chance to trim conifers (in the south of the UK)**

OCTOBER 2015

SUNDAY
25

MONDAY
26

TUESDAY
27

WEDNESDAY
28

THURSDAY
29

FRIDAY
30

SATURDAY
31

Your notes

WEATHER:

PLANTS IN BLOOM

TO DO:

true or false?

'Petunia' is the name given to Asteroid 1227, floating about in our solar system.

(Answer at the bottom of page 163)

PLANT IT

Forcing bulbs for Christmas

There's still time to force bulbs for Xmas – and to make fantastic gifts of them

FYI
Small bags of 'pot toppers' are a cheap way to buy pebbles and stones. Ask at your local garden centre.

Rather than give friends and family amaryllis bulbs still in their boxes at Christmas time, why not pot them up into pretty glass vases of pebbles and stones to adds a personal homemade touch? Get started now and you should have green shoots – maybe flowers – in time for the festive period. Cut flower vases make good vessels as they are deep enough to support large amaryllis bulbs, but if you don't have anything suitable, scout local charity shops for something similar; these glass vases came from IKEA. Near the big day, it is a good idea to add a festive ribbon as a finishing touch.

Bulbs will happily grow in stones, glass chippings or pebbles, as all the goodness they need to flower is contained within the bulb itself

Paperwhites

Paperwhite narcissi also grow well in stones or pebbles. Place a shallow layer of stones in a glass vase and nestle the bulbs closely together. Anchor them down with more stones, leaving the necks protruding.

Water to just below the base of the bulbs and place somewhere cool and light. You should see flowers appear in about six weeks – just in time for Christmas. Their gorgeous snow-white blooms will perfume a room for weeks.

Planting an amaryllis bulb in a glass container

1 Add a heaped teaspoon of aquarium charcoal or a couple of drops of bleach. This is an optional stage but is a good idea, as it'll keep the water sweet.

2 Next, add a shallow layer of stones or pebbles to sit the bulb on. It's best to sit the bulb as low down in the vase as possible, so that it's anchored well.

3 Tease out the roots and place bulb upright in the vase. Add more stones up to the bulb's neck. Gently tap the vase on the table to even out the stones.

4 Water to just below the base of the bulb. Place the vase somewhere cool and light. Keep an eye on the water level – top it up as necessary.

Hyacinths

A glass vase of sphagnum moss is an unusual and attractive way to grow them – place somewhere cold and dark to get the root system going. Water little and often to keep the moss damp. Make sure that you only use 'prepared' bulbs, as these are the ones to use for forcing hyacinths into flowering early.

Plan timing

The exact timings for the growth and development of hyacinths will vary according to the variety being grown. For example, 'Anna Marie' needs eight weeks cool and 18 days inside to bloom (so plant bulbs on 12 October for blooms by Christmas); 'Pink Pearl' however needs 10 weeks of cool conditions followed by 22 days indoors to reach flowering stage (so plant bulbs on 24 Sept). Low temperatures will delay development, so some experimentation may be needed with each variety.

GROW IT

Starting out with fruit

It's time to get fruity! Here's a whistle-stop tour of the different types

A UTUMN IS the perfect time to plant out all manner of fruit trees, bushes, plants and crowns. Roots will grow out in the relatively warm soil through to early winter, allowing plants to romp away when things warm up again next spring.

Most fruit plants are long lived, and will crop for many years. Strawberries are perhaps the quickest to wane, but you'll still get a good three or four years of productivity.

If you've dabbled with veg growing only to find it hard work for little return (you're not alone, many people do!), then fruit may be a better option. Depending on the variety and the growing method you choose, fruit care may be as simple as a spring feed and a bit of pruning in the dormant season.

Tasting a freshly picked strawberry, warmed by the summer sun, is something every gardener needs to experience, so get a small patch on the go. For the best first year harvest seek out plants raised as misted tips (*see below*).

The other fruit on these pages can be planted from now right though winter.

FYI

Soft and top fruit can be grown from winter hardwood cuttings; pinch some prunings from a friend and give it a go

Hassle-free strawberries

Strawberry plants can take a couple of years to reach their cropping potential, but looking for quicker results, consider planting a 'misted tips' continuity collection (←marshalls-seeds.co.uk), which promises heavier yields in the first year.

The collection includes three varieties to extend the harvest – 'Christine' (early), 'Malling Centenary' (main) and 'Fenella' (late), to give the longest picking window through summer. They are produced from unrooted early runners, taken early from the mother plants. They are grown on in mist units for fast establishment, going on to produce larger roots than standard runners. This also encourages flower bud formation in autumn rather than spring, helping to ensure the high first-year yield.

DO IT NOW

Strawberry planting tips

1 Set plants to soak in a root drench of liquid seaweed solution (1 cap to 6litres of water). Strawberries respond particularly well to this tonic. Soak the plants while you prepare the soil.

OTHER FRUITS TO TRY IN THE GARDEN...

Top fruit

Top fruit is simply any variety of fruit produced on a tree rather than a bush. Apples are the obvious choice, but do think about pears, plums, gages, cherries and apricots, peaches and nectarines too. It will take several years to get there, but a well-established, heavy cropping fruit tree is a real asset to the garden.

Most types of fruit tree now come on dwarfing roots, and with a bit of pruning know-how you can grow a fruit tree in even the smallest garden.

Soft fruit

Soft fruit is the term for any berry crop harvested from a bush. Redcurrants, blackcurrants and whitecurrants and gooseberries are all easy to grow in the garden with little fuss.

Heavy crops can be had from plants pruned to just 3ft (1m) or so, so they needn't take up too much space. Blackberries and their hybrids are often classed in this group, but these ramblers are best dealt with separately.

Raspberries

There are two options when it comes to choosing raspberries - summer croppers and autumn croppers.

The latter come highly recommend, particularly if you have strawberries to keep you going through summer. Their pruning is less involved and they require no supports, unlike summer varieties. Of course you can grow both for fresh fruits from June to October.

2 Clear soils of weeds and improve fertility with the addition of plenty of compost or rotted horse manure. Level the site then rake in a balanced feed.

3 For a weed-free bed, lay weed control fabric and peg down or tuck into the soil with a spade blade. Plant through the fabric, 12in (30cm) apart, with 18in (45) or so between rows for easy picking.

Blackberries and hybrids

Less thuggish than the wild bramble and easier to train on wires, fences, arches etc, these cane fruits are a bit too vigorous for small plots and novice gardeners. It may be best to stick with foraging berries from wild plants.

However, new hybrids, such as the Tay berry (a cross of blackberry/raspberry), does make this group a tempting option. Given plenty of space and training, good yields on tidy plants are possible.

PLANT IT

Time to conker the world!

October is the perfect month to start off your own trees from seed

CHILDREN LOVE picking up woodland treasures such as conkers and acorns. They put them in their pockets so that when they get home they can dream of growing massive trees in their parents' gardens.

Unfortunately, invariably these treasures are forgotten about, or they are put into the garden where they just dry out.

If you've always been put off trying to grow a tree from seed, it is not as tricky as you might think. Even if you have a small garden you can keep it in a pot.

If you're wondering where you can track down different native tree seeds then you should contact The Tree Council (☎ 0207 407 9992) which campaigns for better care for all trees. Its website (www. treecouncil.org.uk) offers even more sowing advice for gardeners to follow.

FYI
Remember that named tree or shrub varieties (or 'cultivars') do not come true from seed, but species plants usually do

Alnus seedling (left) from seed sown a year ago, and hawthorn berries (right) for sowing now

Sowing and growing trees in containers

1 Fill a series of clean 3in (7.5cm) pots, or one larger pot, with a seed and cuttings compost, such as John Innes No. 1, and firm gently. Do not overfill – leave a ½in (1cm) gap at the top.

2 Sow larger seeds, such as conkers and acorns single, or three to a 5in (13cm) pot. For medium-sized seeds such as betula, sow approximately 12 seeds per 3in (7.5cm) pot. Scarify acorns with a nail file or sandpaper.

Seed information

Scarifying

If you've collected seeds such as acorns and conkers that have a hard seed coat, you need to rub away at the impermeable coating with some sand paper. Do, however, avoid rubbing down the area near the eye of the seed (this is where the shoot will emerge). By helping break down the surface you will allow moisture to enter the seed and speed up germination. Once you've rubbed the surface, soak the seed in a jar of warm (not boiling) water overnight. Now you're ready to sow.

Extracting seeds

Sorbus, ilex and crataegus hold their seeds in their fruits (berries). To extract these seeds, squeeze the berries until they split and then pop them into a thoroughly washed jam jar filled with water. Leave them to soak and eventually the berry pulp will separate from the seed, Drain the contents through a sieve, tipping the viable seeds back into the jar, ready for sowing. Make sure you use a seed compost such as John Innes No. 1.

Stratifying

Alnus, arbutus, betula and chaenomeles seeds should not be allowed to dry out because they'll fail to germinate when you get around to sowing them. To germinate properly, the seeds need a certain amount of time in the cold. Put collected seed into a sandwich bag and mix with compost that's just moist. Close up the bag and store in the fridge. The seeds should stay there until February, which will allow them a long enough cold period before you sow, again in seed compost.

3 For the large seeds, sprinkle their own depth of compost over the top and gently firm. With medium and fine seeds sieve a dusting of compost on top or top up with vermiculite or horticultural sand.

4 Once you've topped your pot, label it clearly, and water well using the fine rose on your watering can. Leave the pots in a sheltered place such as a coldframe or cool greenhouse until spring.

Masterclass

October

Late containers

Some topical planting ideas to give your garden an autumn glow

THE NIGHTS may be drawing in and the weather getting chillier, but it's not ready quite yet to admit that winter's coming. To start with, give your pots an autumnal theme, using plants that have strong shades of red, orange, purple and gold.

Garden centres these days offer colour all year round, so there's plenty to choose from right now – from golden leaved grasses and mini-chrysanths to jewel-coloured pansies and purple-leaved heucheras.

If you fancy some instant colour to cheer up your patio, look out for whatever is looking good at your local garden centre.

If you want to keep costs down,

simply add a few pansies or cyclamen to an existing pot, and at the same time give it a topdressing of fresh compost.

As the main focal point in this autumn pot we've used a vibrantly coloured *Pennisetum* 'Fireworks'. Pennisetums are normally hardy, but this particular one is on the tender side, so if you're in a cold part of the country, substitute it for a pink-leaved phormium.

		OCTOBER				
S	M	T	W	T	F	S
				1	2	3
4	5	6	7	8	9	10
11	12	13	14	15	16	17
18	19	20	21	22	23	24
25	26	27	28	29	30	31

Clocks go back

Step by step

For this pot you'll need:

- A warm coloured, frost-resistant patio pot at least 12in (30cm) across at the top
- Multipurpose compost
- Crocks for drainage, or polystyrene chunks
- 1 x *Pennisetum* 'Fireworks' (1)
- 1 x *Heuchera* 'Marmalade' (2)
- 3 x Blue or purple pansies (3)

1 Large pots use lots of compost, so bulk out the volume with chunks of polystyrene (from packing boxes). This will also help to improve drainage.

Top plants

To make an autumn pot for decorating the patio, or as a 'welcome' to visitors outside your front door, use any of the plants listed below. They'll provide colour until the start of winter.

For the centrepiece:
- **Coloured-leaved phormium** *(pictured)*
- **Red-leaved cordyline**
- **Red pennisetum**
- *Elaeagnus pungens* 'Frederici'
- *Acer palmatum* **(choose one with red or gold autumn foliage)**

Mid-height:
- **Red, orange or purple heuchera** (*pictured is 'Delta Dawn'*)
- **Orange, red or purple mini chrysanthemums**
- **Golden sedge**
- *Skimmia japonica* 'Rubella' (red berries)
- *Euonymus alatus* **'Compactus'** (red autumn leaves)

Small and trailing:
- **Black mondo grass** (*Ophiopogon planiscapus*, *pictured*)
- **Golden or cream variegated ivies**
- **Orange, yellow or blue pansies**
- **Red cyclamen**
- **Ornamental kale**
- **Trailing nepeta** (glechoma)
- **Coloured bugle** (*Ajuga reptans*)

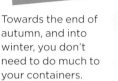

Aftercare

Towards the end of autumn, and into winter, you don't need to do much to your containers. But you should:

- Remember to site them (particularly when they are looking their best) where they will be visible: for example, don't put them on a part of the patio that you can't see from main rooms indoors!
- Water them (*above*) to make sure they don't dry out. Autumn rain doesn't always soak the compost, particularly if the containers are sited under house eaves, or large-leaved plants act as an umbrella and the rain runs off.
- Move them to a position that is more sheltered in bad weather, so the plants don't get battered about.
- Feeding won't hurt! Although the plants do not absorb much in the way of nutrients in late autumn and winter, mixing in some slow-release fertiliser to the compost at planting time will only do some good. If you don't do this, make a few holes with a pencil and drop in a few slow-release fertiliser tablets, available from garden centres.

2 Always use a good quality, fresh multipurpose compost. Start by pouring in enough compost to fill two thirds up the height of the container.

3 Nestle your main plant (here the pennisetum) into the compost. The top of the rootball should be 1-2in (2.5-5cm) below the pot rim.

4 Set your other plants to the side and front of the pot. Low or trailing plants should be set at the edge so they come down the sides of the container.

TRUE OR FALSE FROM p155: **FALSE.** Astronomers have actually named this asteroid 'Geranium'.

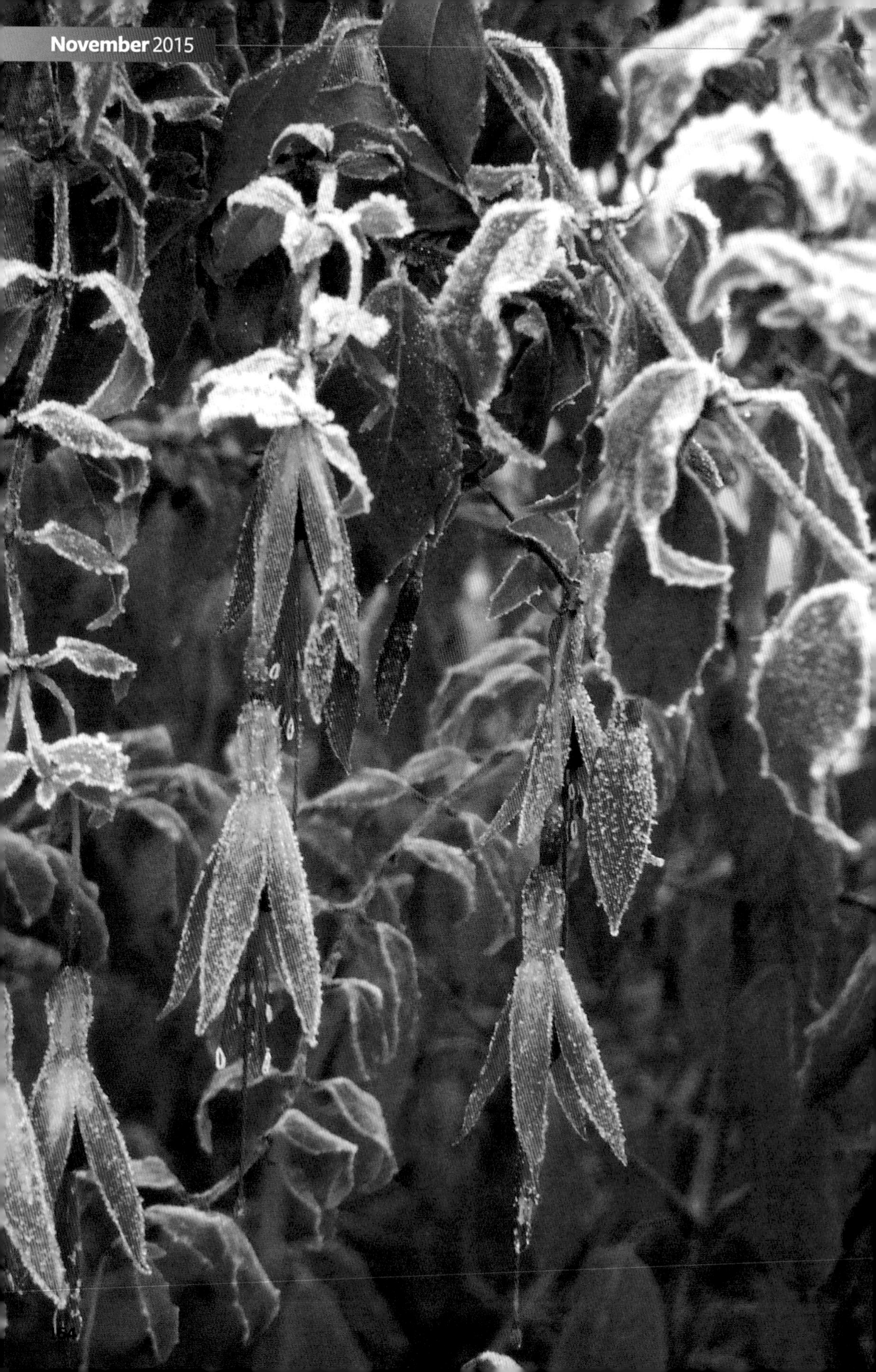

NOVEMBER

Because of reduced daylight hours, there is never much time available for outside garden work in November, so it is a good idea to sit back, take stock and plan ahead. Is the garden too open to all the winds that blow? And can this be improved by the use of windbreaks? On the other hand, is to too sheltered and lacks sunshine? If so, some cutting down or even removal of the causes of shade are necessary.

Tree and shrub leaves are falling rapidly, and wind and rain are on the increase. Tender plants will need protecting from frost, gales and freezing rains.

It is important to move tender or vulnerable plants into the greenhouse, or into a sheltered spot – but if you can't, it is worth wrapping plants or pots *in situ*.

There will still be a colourful display of autumn leaf tints and fruits from plants mentioned in October. Look out, too, for crab apples, sorbus, and autumn/winter-flowering cherries.

◁ *Lingering summer-flowering plants, such as this hardy fuchsia, will often give lots of colour until the frosts of autumn kill off the top-growth*

The garden in
November

This is a gateway into the fascinating interactive world of plants and people. The world's largest geodesic domes contain two distinct biosphere's for you to explore: the Humid Tropical Biome featuring a jungle environment, and the Warm Temperate Biome, featuring plant species from the Mediterranean, South Africa and California. Whilst outside there is a series of landscaped gardens where you can enjoy a diverse collection of plants from the Wild Cornwall section to the terraced tea slopes.

HOW TO GET THERE: Eden is near the Cornish town of St Austell and is well signposted from the main roads. From the car parks, you can either walk down to the visitor entrance and ticket desks or take a free park and ride bus. For details of public transport, visit www.edenproject.com and follow the links.

OPENING TIMES: Open every day except Christmas Eve and Christmas Day. Opening times vary as a result of daylight hours, and the wealth of special events that take place. Consult the website or ring 01726 811911 for specific dates. Every day, the last entry to the Rainforest and Mediterranean Biomes is half an hour before Eden closes.

The Eden Project, Cornwall PL24 2SG

5 top plants for November

1 Yew (*Taxus baccata*) is a British native conifer, grown as a hedging plant. It produces red poisonous berries in autumn.
2 For berries of bright blue, look no further than the evergreen *Viburnum davidii*.
3 The ornamental vine (*Vitis coignetiae*) turns to bright red during autumn.
4 Rose hips can be stunning in the autumn – these are of the hedging rose *Rosa rugosa*.
5 *Cortaderia selloana* 'Sunningdale Silver' is arguably the best of the pampas grasses.

This month in
Gardening
history

■ *14 NOVEMBER 1840*
Claude Monet, famous French impressionist painter and gardener was born. He created the garden at Giverny, famous for its waterlilies, bridge and lake, which he painted many times. Below is *The Water-Lily Pond* (also known as *Japanese Bridge*), which Monet painted in 1899.

■ *21 NOVEMBER 1943*
The first television gardening programme, called *In Your Garden* with C.H. Middleton, was transmitted live from the BBC studios at Alexandra Palace, London.

■ *29 NOVEMBER 1843*
Gertrude Jekyll, influential horticulturist, garden designer, plantswoman and artist was born, at 2 Grafton Street, Mayfair, London. She created more than 400 gardens in the UK, US and across Europe. She died on 8 December, 1932.

NOVEMBER 2015

SUNDAY

1

MONDAY

2

TUESDAY

3

WEDNESDAY

4

THURSDAY

5

FRIDAY

6

SATURDAY

7

SUNDAY

8

AT A GLANCE
JOBS TO DO THIS MONTH

 GENERAL TASKS

- [ ] Continue digging over veg patch and any other empty beds.
- [ ] Make leaf mould from fallen leaves.
- [ ] Order seed catalogues.
- [ ] Clean out bird boxes and tables.
- [ ] Check for anything that's at risk from cold, wind or waterlogging.
- [ ] Last chance to protect tender plants. Lag outside taps to prevent freezing.

 LAWNS

- [ ] Only mow lawns if needed and keep the blades high.
- [ ] Last chance to lay new turf.

 TREES, SHRUBS AND CLIMBERS

- [ ] Plant bare-rooted deciduous trees, shrubs and roses.
- [ ] Take hardwood cuttings of cornus, roses, weigela, buddleja and forsythia.

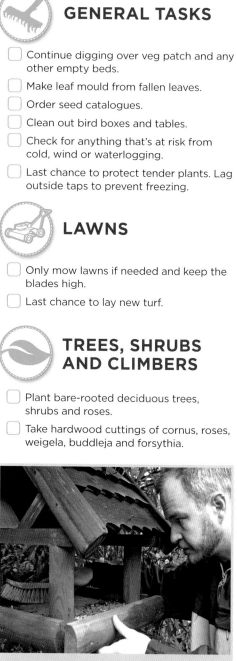

Clean out bird boxes and tables

NOVEMBER 2015

MONDAY

9

TUESDAY

10

WEDNESDAY

11

THURSDAY

12

FRIDAY

13

SATURDAY

14

SUNDAY

15

MONDAY

16

Protect alpine plants from winter rains

Your notes

WEATHER:

PLANTS IN BLOOM:

TO DO:

NOVEMBER 2015

TUESDAY

17

WEDNESDAY

18

THURSDAY

19

FRIDAY

20

SATURDAY

21

SUNDAY

22

MONDAY

23

TUESDAY

24

AT A GLANCE
JOBS TO DO THIS MONTH

 FLOWERS

- [ ] Plant tulip bulbs (*right*) – traditionally between Bonfire night and Christmas.
- [ ] Check stored bulbs, corms and tubers for rot.
- [ ] Start amaryllis into flower.
- [ ] Protect alpines from heavy rain with an open-ended cloche pane of glass.

IN THE GREENHOUSE

- [ ] Continue to sow hardy annuals.
- [ ] Sow sweet peas for overwintering.
- [ ] Keep good air circulation around chrysanthemums to avoid mildew.

CONTAINERS AND PATIOS

- [ ] Move pots into shelter by the house.
- [ ] Ensure pots are standing on pot feet to prevent waterlogging.

 **WHAT TO PRUNE**

- ✓ **Prune deciduous trees and shrubs as they fall into dormancy**
- ✓ **Prune back bush roses by a one third, to avoid wind rock**
- ✓ **Trim summer-flowering heathers**

NOVEMBER 2015

WEDNESDAY

25

THURSDAY

26

FRIDAY

27

SATURDAY

28

SUNDAY

29

MONDAY

30

WEATHER:

PLANTS IN BLOOM:

TO DO:

 true or false?

Before becoming a celebrity gardener, Monty Don was a jewellery specialist, designing gems for the rich and famous.

(Answer at the bottom of page 177)

PLANT IT

Autumn colour

FYI
If a plant is well fed in spring and summer, and receives plenty of moisture in summer, its autumn colour lasts longer

Here are 10 of the best garden plants for brilliant autumn leaves and berries

THERE'S A certain kind of warmth and 'cosiness' to autumn. Wood smoke in the air, a crispness to the mornings, kids playing conkers, and the aroma of the apple sheds! It's a reminder that, yes, summer may be over for another year, but life goes on.

To most gardeners, autumn means one thing – the changing leaf tints on trees and shrubs. OK, there are many woody plants that give a hint of brown and then all the leaves fall off – but there are equally as many of them that change from green to fantastic golden yellows, through to oranges, fiery reds and bright purples.

Then there are the trees and shrubs grown for their autumn berries – dripping with little jewels glinting in the autumn sun.

To have a garden devoid of at least one plant recommended for its autumn leaves is a sad garden indeed. So which plants are recommended for their autumn shows? Here is our top 10 must-have plants.

This Japanese maple (Acer japonicum) has turned into brilliant autumn shades

what makes a leaf change colour?

What actually makes a leaf change colour at this time of year? The effects are brought about by a combination of chemical reactions within the leaf cells. Think of leaves as the 'factories' of the plant. When subjected to sunlight, these factories convert the water and food taken up by the roots into energy – essential for good growth and development. The energy is then carried away to all parts of the plant's system.

At the end of summer the great majority of plants – from trees a hundred feet tall to the prized plants in our garden borders – discard their leaves, but not before they withdraw from them as much of the goodness as they can, for storage in their stems and underground parts. This withdrawal causes the usual green colouring in the foliage to change to one of the many great and brilliant shades so characteristic of the autumn scene.

FIVE FOR AUTUMN LEAVES

Japanese maples (*Acer palmatum*) are indispensable. The finely cut leaves of green, pink, red or purple throughout the growing season are reason enough to grow them, but a few go mad in the autumn, too. 'Bloodgood' has deep reddish purple leaves that turn vivid red in autumn; and 'Sango-Kaku' (which used to be known as 'Senkaki') has fresh green leaves that turn to the brightest of canary yellows.

The smoke bush (*Cotinus coggygria*) is probably the best known in its purple-leaved form 'Royal Purple', which is striking all season. But the species itself has green leaves that turn to shades of red and orange in autumn. It can be pruned hard back annually to restrict its size and stimulate bigger leaves.

Fothergilla major is a slow-growing shrub with bottlebrush-like white flowers in spring before the leaves emerge in early summer. They turn to a brilliant orange-yellow in autumn.

Enkianthus campanulatus produces yellow-bronze flowers in summer, but in the autumn the leaves turn to an amazing display of yellows and reds, and everything in between.

The snowy mespilus (*Amelanchier lamarckii*) is a small tree that certainly gives value for money. It has masses of white, starry flowers in late spring, just ahead of the foliage, which opens to a lovely bronzy colour. And then, at the end of the season, the leaves turn to a fabulous fiery copper.

FIVE FOR AUTUMN BERRIES

Gaultheria mucronata is a low-grower, and thrives on most acid to neutral soils in partial shade. It supplies some of the best garden berries, which last well into winter. Choose from rich red 'Cherry Ripe', lilac-pink 'Lilian', and pink with a deep rose blush 'Rosie'.

Cotoneasters are underrated shrubs for the garden. Many provide a wonderful green backdrop; many others have fantastic autumn leaf colours, and a few are grown specially for their autumn berries. Try 'Rothschildianus', a large shrub with creamy yellow berries; or 'Pink Champagne', which bubbles with berries of blush pink!

Viburnum davidii is without doubt the best shrub for blue berries (not the eating kind); it's a low-growing evergreen with clusters of small oval-shaped berries of deep metallic blue.

Callicarpa bodinieri var. *giraldii* 'Profusion' is the shrub to go for if it's purple berries you're after. It's a super shrub that loves the limelight, and in ideal conditions it produces a bonanza of funky lilac-purple berries that last well after the last leaf drops.

Sorbus (known variously as mountain ash or rowan) is the final choice. *Sorbus decora* is decked with countless clusters of gorgeous glossy red fruits, hanging on dark, pink-tinged stems; and *Sorbus* 'Joseph Rock' looks superb with its mass of pretty pale primrose fruits.

SOW IT

The best of broad beans

Sow overwintering broad beans now for an early crop of pods next summer, says *Amateur Gardening* editor **Tim Rumball**

THE IDEA of sowing or planting any crops this late in the year is to reap an early harvest in spring or early summer. The young plants spend the autumn and winter establishing a good root system, and so get away to a better start as the weather warms up again. With not much else growing at this time, broad beans are a worthwhile crop over the winter, in containers or in the soil.

To succeed you need to sow hardy broad beans (some are tender varieties) – there are several on offer nowadays but the old, reliable standard overwintering variety is 'Aquadulce'. This is quite tall growing, reaching 3ft (90cm) or more, so it needs a good sized container – a large 30litre pot or a veg growing bag. I've tried both, and all the plants grew big and strong.

To get the seeds off to a good start I sow into root trainers or large cell trays filled with multipurpose compost. Set one seed per cell, about an inch below the surface, water well and pop it somewhere warm and bright – a windowsill, or a cold frame will do. Germination is generally very reliable, but watch out for mice – they love pinching the seeds!

I filled my bag and pot with recycled compost refreshed with plenty of well rotted horse manure and some blood, fish and bone fertiliser. In retrospect I think I should have used less manure (too much nitrogen... well rotted garden compost would have been better) – top growth of the plants was dramatic, but they didn't make as many bean pods as I expected. Fresh multipurpose compost on its own would be fine (but costly).

The young beans were planted roughly 8in (20cm) apart each way, and an arrangement of canes tied together with string was erected to support plants as they grew (and

Planting broad beans

1 Sow seeds in November in root trainers filled with multipurpose compost

2 When 6in (15cm) tall, set plants in containers 8in (20cm) apart

3 Water well, provide supports for plants, and protect from cats!

deter cats from using it as a loo!). Young plants should be in the ground by early/mid November – the batch in the picture were very late (February!) but the sheltered growing position meant I got away with it.

Protect plants with fleece if the weather is very cold or snowy. Otherwise these vegetables should need little attention.

"I think I should have used less manure!"

Serious growth will take off in spring, and in a good year you should get pickings by late May. Watch out for blackfly on plant tips as the weather warms – spray with a contact organic insecticide. Pick beans when you can see the swellings along the pods. Harvested small, the beans are firm, tender and sweet, but if you let them go they can get very big – at this point the beans inside the pods develop a thick skin, and the flesh takes on a powdery texture. Blanch and skin each bean before eating.

That's just about it for broad beans. You can sow other varieties to plant in March/April for summer harvest, but there are more rewarding crops than these to be had from the limited space container growing allows.

Sowing seeds...

Sow a hardy variety of broad bean seeds in early November for compact plants to set out later in the month. My plants grew tall, but they didn't produce many beans.

Masterclass

November

Dividing perennials

How to lift and divide perennial plants to manage growth and boost vigour

HERBACEOUS PLANTS that have finished their flowering for the year – and as a consequence are not looking too wonderful just now – can be cut down to make them look tidy in the border.

And now is also the perfect time to divide them.

Plants that are old and bare in the centre, or that have outgrown their space, should be lifted and divided. Some, such as sedums, thrive on being divided every year (yes, really). Others, such as peonies, resent the process and once replanted tend to sit and sulk for several years before they deign to produce flowers.

Use a garden fork to lift the clump, first made loose in the ground by forking all the way around it. Place the clump on a sheet of polythene or tarpaulin.

The division process will take one of three forms (*see next page*). The aim is to split the clump into a number

Dividing this overgrown hemerocallis (daylily) clump will make it more productive

FYI

If you can't divide plants until spring, tag them now, while they are in leaf and visible – in spring they'll look small!

of small, healthy plants. Discard the old centre of the parent plant; the fringes of a mature perennials are always where it is most vigorous.

Before replanting the divisions, revitalise the soil with organic matter, and plant the smaller pieces – ideally in groups of three or five, depending on the amount of available space.

3 ways to divide perennials

Plants that are small, or that have fibrous roots – such as alpines, primulas or this hosta – can often be divided with your hands. Prise the plant apart, in the same way you open up an orange with your fingers.

For larger plants with a congested rootball, you will need to use some tools. It is common practice to use two garden or border forks, back-to-back, to help you prise the plant apart.

Older, woodier plants may have developed thick roots, and these will need severing rather than prising apart. A spade (with a sharpish blade) may be used, or use a pruning saw.

Potting on for spring planting

Sometimes, with the best will in the world, you can't always replant all the little divisions: perhaps you don't have space for them, or other plants currently occupy the space you have in mind for them.

So in this instance pot up the divisions. Pot them into suitably sized pots, using a John Innes No 2 or 3 compost, with a small handful of grit added per pot. Water them in to settle them, and keep them outdoors over winter in a cool but sheltered part of the garden, where they will not dry out completely. Plant out in spring.

NOVEMBER

S	M	T	W	T	F	S
1	2	3	4	5	6	7
8	9	10	11	12	13	14
15	16	17	18	19	20	21
22	23	24	25	26	27	28
29	30					

Plant out broad beans

Bonfire night!

TRUE OR FALSE FROM p171: **TRUE.** Monty and wife Sarah made costume jewellery and traded under the name Monty Don Jewellery.

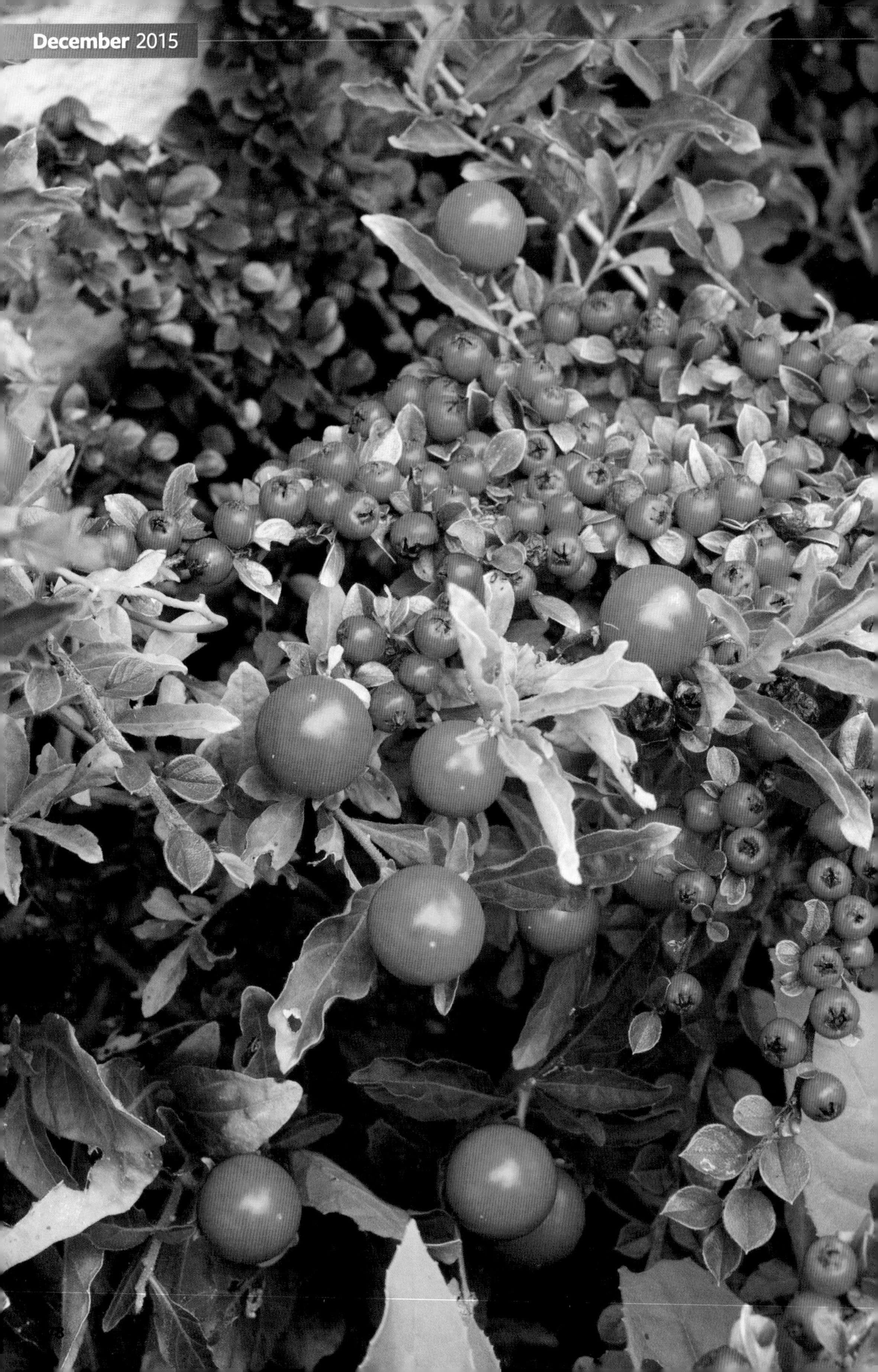

DECEMBER

You may not want to be working outside at this time of year, but luckily there's not a lot to do. Keep an eye on winter protection, and if you have a greenhouse, make sure the heater works.

Whatever the weather in December may be – mild and windy, wet and cold, or foggy and dry – one thing is certain...the nights are long and there is little daylight. Light is very important to plants, and does much to regulate their stages of development.

Few of us use artificial lighting for plants, so it is worth considering using any form of glass, plastic or Perspex covering to protect (or bring on) our plants over winter. All of these materials effectively reduce the amount of light coming in, so they should be kept as clean (free from grime, soil or grease) as possible.

It's time to think about pruning apples and pears, too.

Plants looking good in December include hollies (variegated or berrying types), witch hazels and winter heathers. With Christmas on the doorstep, also look out for the glistening of white mistletoe berries.

◁ *With a distinctly Christmassy feel, much colour can be had in December from berrying plants, such as cotoneaster and winter cherry*

The garden in

December

GARDEN
TO
VISIT

T his is a 65acre (26ha) garden of intoxicating beauty, meticulously crafted and planted, retaining the essence of rural North Devon within a dramatic backdrop of steep wooded valley sides. It is a delight all-year-round, but at this time of year the Winter Garden – specially designed to reflect the best that horticulture has to offer at this bleak time of the year – comes into its own. Conifers and heathers, enormously tough, sit on the northern edge, enjoying the sun to the full.

HOW TO GET THERE: Exit the M5 Southbound Exit at Junction 27, and join the A361 link road signposted Barnstaple/Bideford. At Barnstaple join A39 signposted Bideford (Atlantic Highway), then turn off on the B3232 for Great Torrington. RHS Garden Rosemoor is signposted at Great Torrington and is situated 1 mile south on the A3124 road heading towards Exeter. Car parking is free. For details of public transport, visit www.rhs.org.uk/Gardens and follow the links.

OPENING TIMES: Open every day except Christmas Day. Oct to Mar 10am-5pm; Apr to Sept 10am-6pm. Last admission one hour before closing.

RHS Garden
Rosemoor,
Devon
EX38 8PH

5 top plants
for December

This month in *Gardening* history

1 Poinsettias are popular indoor plants for Christmas – these days there are variegated and cream varieties as well.
2 Perfect winter conservatory plants, paperwhite narcissi are highly fragrant.
3 *Hippeastrum* 'Red Lion' is a gorgeous indoor bulbous plant with large red flowers.
4 *Cyclamen coum* is one of the nicest of the hardy winter-flowering cyclamen.
5 The conifer *Calocedrus decurrens* 'Berrima Gold' is glinting in the winter sunshine.

■ **7 DECEMBER 1817**
Ex-master of HMS Bounty, Vice Admiral William Bligh (*above*) died. The Blighia fruit is named after him.

■ **21 DECEMBER**
An old adage says that we should plant shallots on the shortest day (21 Dec). They should then be ready for harvesting on the longest day (21 June).

■ **21 DECEMBER 1864**
Edwin Hillier bought a nursery and floristry business in Winchester, Hampshire. It grew to become a multi-million pound nursery and garden centre business – Hillier & Sons.

■ **25 DECEMBER 1800**
The first Christmas tree in Britain was erected at Queen's Lodge, Windsor, by Queen Charlotte.

DECEMBER 2015

TUESDAY

1

WEDNESDAY

2

THURSDAY

3

FRIDAY

4

SATURDAY

5

SUNDAY

6

MONDAY

7

TUESDAY

8

AT A GLANCE
JOBS TO DO THIS MONTH

 GENERAL TASKS

- [ ] Put salt on icy paths but keep it away from nearby plants.
- [ ] Clean fallen leaves from gutters.
- [ ] Order seed catalogues.

 LAWNS

- [ ] Don't walk on lawns if it's frosty as you'll kill the grass (*pictured*).
- [ ] Rake up any fallen leaves – lack of light will cause the lawn to die off.

 IN THE GREENHOUSE

- [ ] Check bulbs, corms and tubers in storage, and discard any that are showing signs of rotting.
- [ ] Bring forced bulbs indoors into the warmth and light.
- [ ] Pot up lilies for flowers in the spring.
- [ ] Check that greenhouse heaters are still working – clean up wicks, check electric cabling, empty tanks and fill with fresh paraffin; adjust thermostats accordingly.
- [ ] Reduce watering to a minimum.
- [ ] Bring bay trees under cover to protect them from the cold.

DECEMBER 2015

WEDNESDAY

9

THURSDAY

10

FRIDAY

11

SATURDAY

12

SUNDAY

13

MONDAY

14

TUESDAY

15

WEDNESDAY

16

Choose your Christmas tree – not too soon or the needles will drop, but not too late or you'll miss the better trees!

Your notes

WEATHER:

PLANTS IN BLOOM:

TO DO:

DECEMBER 2015

THURSDAY

17

FRIDAY

18

SATURDAY

19

SUNDAY

20

MONDAY

21

TUESDAY

22

WEDNESDAY

23

THURSDAY

24

AT A GLANCE
JOBS TO DO THIS MONTH

FLOWERS

- [ ] Protect herbaceous plants vulnerable to frost, such as penstemons, by covering the crowns with a layer of bracken or straw.
- [ ] Continue to cut down perennials, weed and tidy borders when the weather permits.
- [ ] Continue to clear fallen leaves from the crowns of alpines and rock gardens.
- [ ] Sow alpine seeds and leave pots outside, with a sheet of glass over the top to protect from the wet – the cold will break seed dormancy.

TREES, SHRUBS AND CLIMBERS

- [ ] Only plant if the soil isn't frozen.
- [ ] Check newly planted trees haven't been lifted by the frost.
- [ ] Protect newly planted evergreens with a windbreak made from posts and fleece (*pictured*).

- [ ] Choose your Christmas tree: Norway spruce is traditional but Nordmann Fir has better needle retention.

WHAT TO PRUNE

- ✓ **Renovate deciduous shrubs like forsythia and philadelphus**
- ✓ **Prune deciduous trees and shrubs for health and shape**

DECEMBER 2015

FRIDAY

25

SATURDAY

26

SUNDAY

27

MONDAY

28

TUESDAY

29

WEDNESDAY

30

THURSDAY

31

 *your notes*

WEATHER:

PLANTS IN BLOOM:

TO DO:

true or false?

Top TV celebrity Alan Titchmarsh, famous for his daytime chat show and his 'ground-breaking' gardening programmes, once asked the editor of this book "How can I get on the telly?".

(Answer at the bottom of page 189)

SOW IT

Grow hellebores for real Christmas presence!

FYI
Helleborus lividus from the Mediterranean grows to just 15in (38cm) or so, and is best grown in pots

You may wish to clear borders of detritus and debris now, but make sure you leave your hellebores to look their best

T HERE IS no such thing as a really ugly hellebore. These plants are so attractive, and generous in their flowering at a time when many other plants are snoozing their way through winter. And there's such a choice to be had.

One hellebore with a beautiful name is the Christmas rose, or *H. niger*. Of course, it's not a rose at all; it is so called because of its resemblance to the single wild dog rose.

It's the original hellebore from which many varieties have been bred, but the white, sometimes creamy flowers appear any time from late December through to April. One variety worth looking out for is the appropriately named 'Christmas Carol'.

But by far the most popular hellebores are the Lenten roses, forms of *H.* x *hybridus* (still called *H. orientalis* by many). These garden hybrids come in a vast array of shapes, sizes and colours, and are definitely worth seeking out. The flowers are from white and yellow, through apricots and pinks, to maroons and near blacks, with single colours, spots, double flowers and frilled blooms all vying for attention.

One of the most robust of hellebores is *H. argutifolius*. It's a handsome brute, reaching 15in (38cm) high, and produces prickly grey-green leaves all year round. Clusters of pale green cup-shaped flowers appear without fail from January through to March. Breeders have also introduced the variety 'Silver Lace', whose sharply toothed leaves have a fine, lacy pattern.

Once the hellebore bug has bitten, many gardeners move on to the even more choice types. For example, a tender little thing all the

After a few hellebores, you could get the bug!

way from Majorca is *H. lividus*. Given protection in winter in a cold greenhouse it will produce glossy deep green leaves with creamy veins. The winter flowers are cup-shaped, creamy green with a pinky purple blush.

Originating from southern Turkey, *H. vesicarius* has small, bell-shaped flowers and bright green leaves. Good, too, is the colouring of *H.* x *sternii* which has large serrated purple-tinged leaves. It is evergreen and bears the characteristic lime green flowers in spring.

Finally, 'stinking hellebore' is the unfortunate name given to *H. foetidus* – which is a pity as it is a beautiful plant. It's a tough customer with strikingly dark green evergreen leaves. Clusters of green flowers hang from flower stems in winter, often blooming sporadically until well into summer. It grows to 18in (45cm) high.

HELLEBORE PLANTS

1 The Christmas rose (*Helleborus niger*)

2 The Lenten rose (*Helleborus x hybridus*)

3 *Helleborus* 'Potter's Wheel'

4 'White Spotted Lady' (*Helleborus x hybridus*)

5 *Helleborus* 'Pacific Frost'

6-point plan for succeeding with hellebores

1 They'll grow quite happily in a semi-shaded site under trees and shrubs, but all hellebores hate cold winds, so don't plant them in exposed places. Also, the classic moist but well-drained soil is ideal. Hellebores hate waterlogged soil.

2 Add plenty of organic matter – well-rotted garden compost and leafmould is fantastic – to the soil at planting time.

3 Mulch around the bases of plants with the same organic matter every spring.

4 Remove any leaves that are affected with black spot. The disease can spread and kill the plant.

5 Remove old leaves when they look ragged in late spring or summer (*left*), to reduce the chance of black spot, and to enable you to see the flowers more clearly.

6 With any *H. argutifolius* it's best to prune out the flowering stems as the blooms fade to encourage more flowers.

Hellebore facts

■ Hellebore flowers more often than not droop down, requiring a great degree of flexibility in the gardener to see them at their best. But this is because the flowers generally open at a time of year when the weather can damage the pollen. Think about that next time your knees creak!

■ If hellebores were having friends around for Christmas, clematis and buttercups would come knocking at the door!

■ In the 17th century hellebores were regarded as a suitable treatment for depression and insanity.

■ The Scandinavians love hellebores and often use them as Christmas decorations. Try floating some flowers in a shallow bowl of water, add a couple of floating candles and stand back. Gorgeous!

Masterclass

December

Bare root benefits

December is the cheapest time of year to plant trees, shrubs, roses, fruit and hedging

GARDENING PROJECTS tend to boil down to two factors – time and money. When planning a new planting scheme for the garden, be it trees, shrubs, hedging, roses, fruit patches, orchards or perennial displays, you have to weigh up the time it will take for the display to reach maturity against the price of the plants. The bigger/older the plant, the higher the cost, but the sooner you'll reap the rewards.

Tighter household budgets means that bigger plants are becoming a luxury, but if you're prepared to wait a few years for plants to mature, you can slash your garden spend by choosing bare root plants.

Their name says it all: bare roots are supplied without pots or soil. While pot-grown plants can be bought at any time of year, bare roots must be dug up at the nursery and planted in the garden during their winter dormancy. This is usually November to March but timings depend on local weather conditions at the nursery, so liaise with your chosen supplier.

They aren't much to look at on delivery – often just a bundle of 'sticks' with roots attached, but don't let that disappoint. They will soon establish and within six years or so will have caught up with their container-grown counterparts.

For the widest choice, seek a specialist mail order/online retailer and order in December. Then follow the planting tips on the next page for success.

FYI
Inconvenient delivery time? No problem. Set plants in a trench and cover roots with soil until ready to plant

Bare roots are usually supplied with roots wrapped in plastic – sometimes packed with compost, but often not!

DECEMBER

S	M	T	W	T	F	S
		1	2	3	4	5
6	7	8	9	10	11	12
13	14	15	16	17	18	19
20	21	22	23	24	25	26
27	28	29	30	31		

Plant shallots   *Christmas!*

PLANTING BARE ROOTS TREES

1 Assess the size of the roots on your new tree and dig a hole large enough to be able to spread them out in the bottom of it.

2 Before setting in place, trim off any damaged roots just behind where they are broken, and cut back any very long roots.

If you want a more unusual variety of tree or a fruiting variety on a larger rootstock, these tend to be available only as bare-root trees – and specialist suppliers will have the widest selection.

Also, if you want to train a fruit tree into a fan, espalier or cordon, a bare root tree is usually the best and cheapest way to start. Plum trees are particularly good bare root options in winter as container-grown plums can be difficult to establish during the cold season.

No matter what variety you choose, ornamental or fruiting, follow the planting steps below. The cherry tree here is to be trained as a fan against fencing. For open grown trees, drive a stake into the planting hole before setting the tree in place and tieing in.

3 Before filling in the hole, lay a cane across it to check the planting level is such that the soil mark on the stem matches the level of the surrounding soil.

4 Fill the hole in stages, treading down as you go; this will knock out air gaps, and ensure good soil-to-root contact. Water well, and apply a mulch around base.

Why choose bare roots?

- You'll pay less for the same size plants
- Easy to transport, carry and plant
- Wider selection of plant varieties available
- No need for immediate planting: plants can be heeled into a trench until you are ready (*above*)
- Winter weather takes care of watering in the first few months, meaning less aftercare will be needed

Step by step — Bare root hedging

1 Stand plant roots in a bucket of water to soak while you set out a string planting line. For a double row hedge, set out two lines spaced 18in (45cm) apart.

2 Lay out plants along the row; stagger plants along double rows. Cut a piece of 18in (45cm) cane to act as a spacer and dig out your first planting hole.

3 Set each plant in its hole at the same depth as the soil mark at the base of the stem. Tread in as you backfill the hole. Water well when all plants are in.

TRUE OR FALSE FROM p185: **TRUE.** In 1977 Alan and the editor of this book, Graham Clarke, shared an office on the 25th floor of a high-rise block on London's South Bank, from where *Amateur Gardening* magazine was produced (at the time). Alan had been wanting to break into television so asked the room if anyone had any ideas. Graham offered him a letter just received from the BBC, asking for experts to get in touch – and the rest is history!

Pedigree®

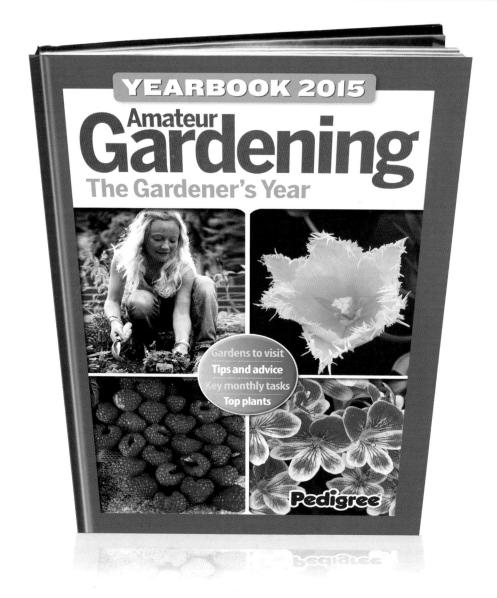